Path to

Enlightenment
The Golden Throne

Nasrin Safai

BOOK II

Waves of Bliss Publishing

Book design: Yantra Design Group, Inc.

Photography: ©Patsy Balacchi

Diagrams created by Theresa Martin, Michael Kopel, Tonia-Maria Pinheiro

Path to Enlightenment, The Golden Throne, Book II. Waves of Bliss Publishing, 2008.
ISBN 978-0-9821302-1-6
Library of Congress Number: 2008938879

Waves of Bliss Publishing, Jeffersonville, VT 05464.
To order books:
 Email: Nasrin@WavesOfBliss.com
 Website: www.wavesofbliss.com/books

Other books by Nasrin Safai:
Path to Enlightenment, The Pillar of Light, Book I. Waves of Bliss Publishing 2008.

Path to Enlightenment, The Seed of Life, Book III. Waves of Bliss Publishing 2008.

Gifts from Ascended Beings of Light: Prayers, Meditations, Mantras and Journeys for Soul Growth – Gifts I.
Agapi Publishing, 2003.

Gifts of Practical Guidance for Daily Living: Protection, Healing, Manifestation, Enlightenment – Gifts II.
Waves of Bliss Publishing, 2005.

Gifts from the Masters of Light: Journeys Into the Inner Realms of Consciousness – Gifts III.
Waves of Bliss Publishing, 2005.

Gifts of Wisdom and Truth from the Masters of Light: Tools for Clearing,
Release, Abundance and Empowerment – Gifts IV. Waves of Bliss Publishing, 2005.

Altered States, Biographies & Personal Experience, Body Mind & Spirit, Chakras, Channeling, Consciousness: Awareness & Expansion, Creation Spirituality, Daily Meditation, Everyday Spirituality, God, Meditation & Prayer, New Age, Origin & Destiny of Individual Souls, Science & Religion, Spiritual Teachers, Spirituality, Self Help, The Self.

Printed in the United States of America.

This book is dedicated
to the Thrones of Light
and the Great Beings
who reside upon these Thrones.

This Book is also dedicated
to all of you in gratitude
for your patience and perseverance
on the Path of Light.

TABLE OF CONTENTS

To Enhance Your Reading Experience xi

The Great Invocation xv

Preface xvi
    The Golden Throne xvii

Introduction 2
    Twin Flames 4
    Templates and Blueprints 8
    Divine Plan 9
    Blueprint of the Divine Will 12
    Personal and Planetary Grids 13
    Light Grids and Candle Grids 15
    Releasing Pain and Struggle 17
    Karma and Karmic Entanglements 18
    Free Will and Karmic Entanglements 19
    Thrones of God 20
    Undifferentiated Source 24
    Paramatman Light 24
    The Throne of Absolute 25
    The Seven Rays 26
    Framework 28

Chakra System 34

Chapter Structure 37

CHAPTER I: RELEASE BETRAYAL AND RESTORE GOD-UNITY   38

Template for Release of Betrayal, Bondage, Enslavement and the Union of Twin Flames to Bring Joy and God-Unity — by Archangel Michael

CHAPTER II: THE GOLDEN THRONE   46

Receiving the Blueprint of Divine Will in the Presence of the Golden Throne — by Jeshua Ben Joseph.

CHAPTER III: KARMA AND KARMIC ENTANGLEMENT   54

Release of Karma and Karmic Entanglements to Realize our Divinely Ordained Mission — by Goddess Hecate.

CHAPTER IV: RELEASING NEGATIVITY   60

Releasing Negative Energies to Gain Higher Light — by St. Germain.

CHAPTER V: TRUTH AND NEGATIVITY   68

Finding Truth through the Release of Negativity at Global Scale — by Metatron.

CHAPTER VI: FORGIVENESS   76

Prayer for Forgiveness and Release of Karmic Entanglement — by Metatron.

CHAPTER VII: REJUVENATION   88

Merging the Red Life Force Energy of Earth with Pure White Light and Embracing the Feminine Creative Force — by Metatron.

CHAPTER VIII: PARAMATMAN LIGHT   96

Calling for the Descent of Paramatman Light to Cleanse Earth and the Five Elements — by Metatron.

CHAPTER IX: ALCHEMY OF HEALING, PROTECTION AND MANIFESTATION   100
Alchemical Grid for Healing, Protection and Manifestation
with Mother Mary, Quan Yin, Archangels Michael, Metatron,
Uriel and Raphael – by Metatron.

CHAPTER X: LORDS OF LIGHT AND THE CREATIVE FORCE   112
Invoking the Lords of Light and Clearing the Five Body System
to Embrace the Creative Force of Divine Mother – by Metatron.

CHAPTER XI: PROTECTION AND TRANSMUTATION   122
Grid of Light for Release of Anger, Fear, Pain and Struggle
– by Metatron.

CHAPTER XII: ABUNDANCE AND PROSPERITY   130
The Divine Mother's Prosperity and Abundance Magnification
Grid of Light – by Divine Mother and Goddess Hecate.

CHANNELING INDEX   142

BIBLIOGRAPHY   145

ACKNOWLEDGEMENTS   147

ABOUT THE AUTHOR   148

OTHER BOOKS BY NASRIN SAFAI   149

KEY TERMS

CHAPTER I: RELEASE BETRAYAL AND RESTORE GOD-UNITY
CREATOR MIND; MIND OF GOD
ORIGINAL DIVINE TEMPLATE
DIVINE MISSION
PERSONALITY ASPECTS
TWIN FLAMES
ETERNAL FLAME
FLAME OF GOD-UNITY
ARCHANGEL MICHAELS'S MANTLE OF BLUE LIGHT
TEMPLATE FOR DIVINELY ORDAINED MISSION

CHAPTER II: THE GOLDEN THRONE
THRONE OF I AM THAT I AM
ZOROASTER
ORIGINAL BLUEPRINT OF DIVINE WILL
GOLDEN THRONE OF YHWH
PILLAR OF LIGHT
TWENTY-FOUR ELDERS
ANCIENT OF DAYS
SANAT KUMARA
THOUSAND PETALED LOTUS
GOD-SELF

CHAPTER III: KARMA AND KARMIC ENTANGLEMENT
KARMA AND KARMIC ENTANGLEMENTS
FEMININE ASPECT, MASCULINE ASPECT
ORIGINAL BLUEPRINT OF DIVINELY ORDAINED MISSION
FIVE ELEMENTS

CHAPTER IV: RELEASING NEGATIVITY
THRONE OF UNDIFFERENTIATED SOURCE
SEVEN MIGHTY ELOHIM
GREAT SILENT WATCHERS
COHAN AND MAHA COHAN OF THE RAYS
VIOLET FLAME
ASCENSION DAY
LORDS OF LIGHT
GUARDIANS OF LIGHT
98,000 YEAR CYCLE OF LIGHT

CHAPTER V: TRUTH AND NEGATIVITY
WESAK AND LORD BUDDHA
UNIVERSAL TRUTH
CRITICAL MASS AWAKENING
SEVEN-YEAR CYCLE
DIVINE WILL

CHAPTER VI: FORGIVENESS
PRAYER FOR FORGIVENESS AND
RELEASE OF KARMIC ENTANGLEMENTS
FREE WILL
TO HOLD THE IMAGE OF PERFECTION
MICROCOSM AND MACROCOSM

Chapter VII: Rejuvenation
Red Life Force
Red Earth Energy
Pink Light of Divine Love
Pure White Light
Twelve Petaled Lotus of the Heart
Aspects of the Divine Mother
Elementals
The Trinity
Creative Force
Goddess Hecate
Goddess Pele

Chapter VIII: Paramatman Light
Paramatman Light
Atman
Spiritizing Matter
Materializing Spirit
Oneness and Duality

Chapter IX: Alchemy of Healing, Protection and Manifestation
Alchemy
Citron-Green Ray of Mental Clarity
Emerald-Green Ray of Truth and Hope
Deep Dark Jade-Green Ray of
    Physical Substance/Essence
Deep Dark Nile-Blue Ray of Protection
Turquoise-Blue Ray of Power
Aquamarine-Blue Ray of Divine Power and Mercy

MANIFESTATION
FIFTH DIMENSIONAL ENERGIES

CHAPTER X: LORDS OF LIGHT AND THE CREATIVE FORCE
FEMININE ENERGY – CREATIVE FORCE
    OF DIVINE MOTHER
GODDESS ENERGIES IN NATURE
UNION OF LIGHT AND DARK
LORDS OF LIGHT
CHRIST MAITREYA
CYLINDER OF LIGHT

CHAPTER XI: PROTECTION AND TRANSMUTATION
GREAT SILENT WATCHER
ANGELS OF THE FOUR DIRECTIONS
TURQUOISE-BLUE BUBBLE OF LIGHT
SERVING BY TRANSMUTING PLANETARY DROSS

CHAPTER XII: ABUNDANCE AND PROSPERITY
THIRTEEN ASPECTS OF THE DIVINE MOTHER
UNLIMITED ABUNDANCE OF THE UNIVERSE
"ASK AND YOU SHALL RECEIVE."
RECOGNIZING SELF-WORTH
POWER OF TRANSMUTATION AND RELEASE OF DARKNESS

To Enhance Your Reading Experience

This book is written as a multi-layer exercise. Reading this book affects you at many conscious and subconscious levels. In order to enhance your experience, please follow these recommendations:

Start by saying;

- *"In the name of Light, in the name of the I Am That I Am, in the name of YHWH, in the name of Undifferentiated Source, in the name of Paramatman, in the name of Divine Mother and the Thrones of Absolute, Creation and the Feminine Principle, I ask to receive the highest benefit from this book at conscious and subconscious levels. I call upon my Personal Guides and Guardian Angels to be present through the course of reading this book. I invite the Angelic Forces of Light, the Masters of Light and the Great Beings of Light to administer to me the highest benefit from their energy and their teachings through this book."*

- Read the Introduction carefully. Key terms and topics have been explained in the Introduction to enhance your experience of the chapters. Familiarity with these terms can improve your understanding and accelerate your ability to incorporate the teachings in your life. If you walk away with a good knowledge of the Introduction, you would have accelerated yourself on the Path to Enlightenment.

- Keep an open mind. Some of the concepts may be new or different from conventional teachings. If something causes you confusion, continue to persevere and be patient. Things are explained in further detail throughout the book. The blanks will most likely be filled by the time you finish the book. If you need more information to augment what is presented here, please read the books in the *Gifts* series by Nasrin Safai and visit www.wavesofbliss.com.

- It is preferable that you begin by reading *Book I* of this series before *Book II.* However, if you have been led here and you feel inclined to follow your instincts, continue on as there are no coincidences, the reason may be revealed to you in time. I would ask you to persevere and read each section more carefully.

- Patience and perseverance are two important qualities for anyone intent on walking a spiritual path. The path of spiritual evolution requires one to contend with a steady climb at the best of times and a roller coaster ride at many others.

- After you read this book from cover to cover, you may still feel that you have not fully understood everything. Do not be concerned, as a period of time for introspection and reflection will bring things to focus. The moment you pick up any one of these channeled books, you begin to walk with the Masters and receive their teachings. At first you may assimilate the materials at subconscious levels. In time, you will begin to consciously understand their wisdom. You may surprise yourself as to how much of this wisdom you retain and use in your everyday life.

- It is my intention to present you with information and materials directly given by the Masters whom I channel. The Masters feel that understanding the subject consciously and energetically through them, as the source, will help the assimilation process. Once you have made your connection with them, and assimilate their teachings, they will lead you to more on that subject, when you ask for it. In that way, you will be lead to what is most pertinent and beneficial for you without confusion or delays. However, for those of you interested in reading more on some of these topics, I provide a short bibliography at the end of the book. These external sources have been mentioned in my *Gifts* series books with greater detail at pertinent points in the text.

- Most chapters contain exercises which are meant to be repeated for twenty two days or for the entire month. As you read each chapter, focus on visualizing the components of each exercise and intend that the energy of the grid of Light, candle grid, invocation or the advice given by the Masters stay with you until fully anchored. Intend that you receive everything you need from each exercise. Ask that the Great Beings invoked continue to bless you with their presence and their gifts during and after you read the book. Later, you can go back to those exercises which call to you and perform them for the recommended period. Be aware however, that you are accelerating yourself enormously. The information in this book was brought to us in the course of two years. Each exercise was intended to be practiced for a minimum of twenty two days or longer. Be patient and gentle with yourself and listen to your instincts. You may need to set the books aside for a while to give yourself a chance to process and to purge. Allow the natural ebb and flow of the energies to help you assimilate the information.

At an especially critical phase of my spiritual evolution, I came across a small book of fourteen short chapters. I was told by the Masters that I would need to anchor the energies in a certain way in different parts of the world. Therefore, the Masters wanted me to read each part for the first time, only when I arrived at the appointed location. This instruction added to my curiosity. I figured that it was not a big deal. I could read it once and then read it again when I reached each destination. However, that was not to be. The book would disappear at different intervals in various places and reappear again. I had missed their point. I listened to the guidance but did not really hear or absorb the importance of the guidance. I only became wise to the pattern after the third round when the book which had disappeared from my bedside made its appearance in my suitcase. I understood the importance of the procedure only after the reading and anchoring of the book was complete. The object of the exercise was to anchor the information in its most pristine and potent manner, by allowing my body to receive and transmit it at the appointed location, without tasking my body to extraneous overload.

My point and the moral of this story is that you too will be reading and anchoring the energies held in this book and the others in this series. Allow the Masters to help you do what is most beneficial for you and through you. Understand that you are held and embraced in the love and consciousness of your Guides, the Angelic Forces and Masters who know what is good for you and are happy to guide you to attain it. To help them do their best on your behalf, clearly express your intentions, surrender to receive the guidance, accept that the outcome is Divinely orchestrated and offer your willingness to be of service to the Light. The Universe will take care of the rest.

THE GREAT INVOCATION

From the point of Light within the mind of God
Let Light stream forth into the minds of men.
Let Light descend on Earth.

From the point of Love within the Heart of God
Let Love stream forth into the hearts of men.
May Christ return to Earth.

From the center where the Will of God is known
Let purpose guide the little Wills of men -
The purpose which the Masters know and serve.

From the center which we call the race of men
Let the Plan of Love and Light work out
And may it seal the door where evil dwells.

Let Light and Love and Power
Restore the plan on Earth.

Christ Maitreya, the World Teacher, and the Masters of Wisdom
highly recommend that we recite the prayer of The Great Invocation
daily. It transmits the energies of great Light, peace and harmony.

PREFACE

This is the second book of a series intended to offer tools to accelerate you on the Path to Enlightenment. The tools are given to us by the Ascended Masters, our sisters and brothers in Light. Their guidance is brought forth by me, Nasrin, through channeled messages. These messages have been derived from advice given by the Masters to seekers during private channeling sessions and life readings. These are people, like you, from all walks of life, who have asked questions and received guidance relevant to and applicable in all our lives. The information was received from 2006 to 2008. Parts were then compiled into newsletters which were posted on my website with some modifications. I was guided by the Masters to turn these into books, with greater detailed definition of terms, to provide a framework for the serious students on the Path.

The information presented in all the books in this series is channeled. I am a channel. I allow my body to be the vehicle for the delivery of information by the Masters from the Higher Realms. These realms are the abode of the Ascended Masters and are places of higher knowledge and wisdom. I retrieve this knowledge by raising my Quotient of Light and the Masters deliver it by lowering theirs. Both require sacrifices and much work, yet I believe, as the Masters do, that the end justifies the means.

The objective for *Path to Enlightenment; Book I*, was to awaken and align the readers to their Divine Mission, the first critical step on the path to Enlightenment. The meditational exercises in Book I prompted the reader to actively seek and live that Mission on Earth. The first step was the opening of the Third Eye for greater perception of reality and connection with the Higher Realms. We moved on from there to open the chakras, or energy centers, of the body. This brought greater understanding of the five layers of our Energy Body. These layers constitute our Five Body System. Awareness of these bodies and their re-connection to the physical body promoted heightened sensitivity, intuitive abilities and inner sight. As a result, a greater intuitive connection between us, in the third dimensional reality and the Masters in the Higher Realms, was re-established. Once our energy bodies were filled with Light, we were brought to the Throne of the I Am That I Am, God in Form. We were able to reconnect with the Presence of the I Am after eons of time in separation. We continued to build on this connection by opening ourselves further to the realms of the unknown to retrieve greater knowledge and wisdom from the Masters. This wisdom brought us healing and self-empowerment, courage and fortitude to know that we are not alone, that we are loved and the emptiness we sometimes feel in our hearts is the result of our longing for Oneness. The emptiness can be filled and the longing quenched when we realize our higher purpose and fulfill our Divine Mission. Deep down we were touched by the memory that there is more to this life than meets the eyes. Book I offered us a chance to bring all of that veiled knowing to the surface.

THE GOLDEN THRONE

The objective for *Path to Enlightenment, Book II, the Golden Throne,* is to move to the next set of steps along the path to Enlightenment. This next set of steps involves finding ways to live in this world in peace and harmony, untouched by distractions and unmoved by greed, anger and fear. In Book II, the Masters bring us tools for acceleration by freeing us from the delays and distractions of this density which lead to bondage of the body, mind and emotions.

Through applying these tools, we will be able to increase our Quotient of Light. Once raised, it is of equal importance to maintain that Higher Light in order to actively change our lives and our world for the better. By increasing our Quotient of Light, we are able to reach the Golden Throne of YHWH (Yah-weh), also known as the Throne of Grace. This Throne resides at the twenty-second dimension of reality, where Light is more brilliant. Golden Shimmering Light fills this Realm. The Presence of YHWH is seated at this Throne. Twenty-four Great Beings of Light called the Elders, also known as the Ancient of Days, are seated in a circle around the Throne. Four creatures are standing guard at the four directions; one with the face of a lion, the second a horse, the third an eagle and the fourth an ox. The twenty-four Elders sing the song of *"Holy, Holy, Holy is the Lord God of Hosts."* With each chant of the Holy name, Bright Light pulses through the Throne and spreads in every direction.

The Golden Throne of YHWH will play a greater role in the destiny of the planet and in the lives of those in service to the Light. The dispensation has been issued from the Hierarchies of Light to make the energy of this Throne more accessible to the multitudes and masses than it has been for eons of time. Through the guidance of the Masters, we have the Grace to touch and be touched by this Throne. We will be able to serve humankind by spearheading the anchoring of the energies of YHWH in this third dimensional reality. Our greater individual growth and evolution will benefit all souls living upon this planet and the planet herself. Mother Earth is also striving to grow in her own evolution on the Path to Enlightenment. Our acceleration affects her evolution to Ascension.

I wish you success in your endeavors to greater personal evolution and in service to the Light. Together we shall become the great and mighty force which shall trigger the Earth to accelerate her pace on the Path of Ascension and the collective consciousness of humankind to realize its divinity.

Nasrin Safai
August 29, 2008
Miami Beach, Florida USA

"I slept and dreamt that life was joy.
I awoke and saw that life was service.
I acted and behold, service was joy."

Rabindranath Tagore, Indian Sage

INTRODUCTION

Book I awakened us to our Divine Mission and provided direction to pursue that mission. Book II takes us a step further by clearing the path for the accomplishment of that Divine Mission.

In Book II, the Masters will guide us to raise our Quotient of Light and maintain that Light while in the density of the third dimension. Through the chapters that follow, the Ascended Masters provide us with the required tools and the necessary knowledge, wisdom and understanding to be successful in this endeavor. These tools also clear the cobwebs and brush off the dust and debris from many lifetimes of forgetfulness and help us free ourselves from the burden of dross. They help us gain mental clarity and emotional stability to avoid further karmic entanglements, delays and distractions.

To properly apply the tools provided, and for a better understanding of the teachings, I offer a brief explanation of several terms and concepts in this Introduction. These explanations have grown out of my own understanding of the terms used by the Masters, while I channel for others. The number of hours spent in channeling sessions has grown to well over 10,000 hours in the course of the last two decades.

For as long as I can remember, I have been a seeker on the path. Even before I could focus my energies to become a Channel of the Masters, I kept striving to learn and know more about this field. In the process, many times I have stumbled and fallen, and made leaps and bounds of growth at others. On many occasions I have requested that the Masters give me the ability to learn from the lessons and experiences of others in order to accelerate myself on the path and to be of service by sharing my own experiences with others. I have grown in the understanding of concepts and issues from the perspective of the Masters and the applicable laws accorded to them in the Higher Realms. I have followed the footsteps of the Masters like a child led by a parent and asked many questions. To answer my questions or to appease my curiosity, sometimes the Masters take me to various realms. Some things are explained and others are shown to me. I am then left to make my own conclusions from what I have seen. Over time, I have built a large body of knowledge and information from the teachings of the Masters and my excursions with them. The application of the sum total of my learning, as presented to you, is meant to make life in this third dimensional reality easier and more enjoyable. It aims to clear the path to live our Heaven on Earth. We shall sow the seeds of joy, peace and harmony in the hope that our children and theirs can be given a chance to taste the fruits and grow to create better tomorrows for generations of their descendents. The Masters have sown seeds of change with their blood, sweat and tears and by sacrificing their Heaven to stand by our side on Earth to guide us. They believe that the end justifies the means. We give time and space a chance for greater acceleration as together we begin a journey to greater Light. I therefore present to you a synopsis of some key terms used in the teachings of the Masters throughout this book. I have accumulated this information over the last three decades from the teachings of the Masters and my research in this field guided by the Masters.

TWIN FLAMES

The subject of Twin Flames and soul mates is touched upon by many, understood by few. It is fraught, therefore, with controversy, yet a subject worthy to be addressed as an entire volume unto itself. For the purpose of this book, a brief perusal of the teachings of the Masters will suffice.

The journey begins at the beginning of time, or should I say even before time existed. There was a point in our history where time and space were one. They were not two separate events on the Time-Space Continuum. Both time and space sat together in Oneness on a continuum of Light. At that time, matter too was Light. Light became energy and energy gained density to shape itself into matter. The dictates of Physical Laws are such that the denser the reality, the more polarized the matter becomes. Consequently, for Light to sustain itself in lower dimensional densities, it would need to accept the dictates of polarization. When Light reaches into the density of this third dimensional realm of duality, it is at its most polarized point.

This law also applies to all beings who would wish to incarnate on Earth. A being of Pure Light living in complete Oneness, unaware of any duality or polarity, would experience this change when brought to the density of these lower dimensions. Such a soul, in moving through density, accepts to become polarized. An original soul would, therefore, have to split itself into two equal and exact halves, with each half the twin essence of the other. One half would become the Feminine Polarity and the other, the Masculine Polarity. This is necessary only when a soul comes down to realms of greater density. In Higher Realms, where polarity is not as pronounced, both male and female components are held within one soul. The soul in its original form, or rather non-form, holds both polarities in total Oneness and as such, is androgynous. In the third dimensional realms, because of the pull of gravity and the forces of polarity, an energy encapsulated in matter either has electrical charge and is therefore Masculine or magnetic charge and is Feminine. This applies to human beings and almost all species of animals and plants. Even places and things emit electrical or magnetic charges. For example, Metatron tells us that the East Coast of the United States holds the electrical force and is Masculine by nature and the West Coast holds the magnetic force and is Feminine. The polarity present at these two ends balances the country and the entire North American Continent.

The concept of Twin Flames has its roots in the splitting of the one soul into two halves. The halves known as Twin Flames are bound to find each other, in order to unite and return to Oneness. The Flame of God-Unity is the original Flame of Oneness which has always been illuminated in the heart of the original soul. This Flame also splits into two, with each half as the exact replica or twin of the other. Each half of the Flame takes residence in the heart of the two polarized halves. When the two original souls are united and their Flames are re-ignited together, their journey of separation is over. At the point of their union, the journey back to Oneness can begin.

The Twin Flames on their journey through time and space split further. Each splitting of the soul at these levels is known as soul fragmentation. This does not pertain to the gender of each fragment. Members of both polarities can be incarnated in male or female bodies at any given time. All the soul fragments which are created from further polarization of the electronic polarity are soul mates and all the fragments created from the magnetic polarity are soul mates to each other.

This is how soul mates and Twin Flames are different. Soul mates are alike because they are created or fragmented from the same half, whereas the Twin Flames are created from opposite halves. Therefore, there is a distinct difference between soul mates and Twin Flames. However, in most available literature the two terms are used interchangeably without a distinction.

The Ascended Masters have a special interest in bringing the Twin Flames together because the evolution of each soul depends upon the union of the two split halves or the original Twin Flames. When destiny and the Free Will choices of both halves provide an opportunity for uniting the Twin Flames, the Masters work hard to bring such an event to a successful conclusion.

In essence, a soul would not truly know wholeness unless it finds its Twin Flame, experiences union and breaks the chasm of polarity and duality to return to Unity. However, sometimes the circumstances may only allow a fleeting experience of Oneness. In other cases the meeting of the Twin Flames may not even lead to a romantic relationship. Furthermore, many a romantic or social relationship between Twin Flames has been known to breakdown due to the emotional and mental depth and intensity of the relationship.

Perhaps the most obvious reason is the great degree of polarity which exists between the forces of the magnetic and the electric, or the female and the male, of the species. Men and women are evolving at different rates and through different means on their path of spiritual growth and evolution. In extreme cases, some Twin Flames have fallen so far apart energetically, physically and spiritually, that even if they were to find one another, they would have little or no common ground to form a relationship. In other cases the force of attraction which pulls the Twin Flames together may become overwhelmingly intense; intensely magnetic and intensely electric. It can even lead to near meltdown experiences. In many a case, the two may feel as though they cannot get enough of each other sometimes and at other times they cannot run away from each other fast enough. It is easy to understand that there is a much greater burn-out effect from the coming together of Twin Flames than there is of soul mates. Soul mates, being of the same polarity, walk on common ground and easily see eye to eye. Yet the completion of any soul's journey can be accomplished from the coming together of the Twin Flames and not the soul mates.

The Masters, therefore view any and all possible connections preferable to none, and do everything in their power to help both parties overcome all obstacles and accelerate to a favorable conclusion. Failing that, the Masters have formulated alternate means to assist us on our path in reaching the goal of Enlightenment. One of these alternate means provides us with a shortcut to do away with, or bypass the necessity of the physical presence of a Twin Flame for the evolution of soul fragments. To create this shortcut, the Masters sought and have been granted the dispensation to call forth the Blueprint for the Original Flame, before it was split into two flames. Consequently, the original flame is called from the Heart of the original soul and placed into the Heart Chakra of each individual soul fragment by the Masters during the meditational exercises given specifically in this book. The Original Flame of Oneness, sometimes called the Flame of God-Unity, and at other times the Eternal Flame, is the Spark of Oneness which illumines the Heart of the Undifferentiated Source. It is undifferentiated because it knows no polarity. There is no differentiation of Light and Dark, male and female, electric and magnetic. The Flame of God-Unity in its perfect original form was placed into the Heart of the original soul as that soul came to manifest form and before it split. The Ascended Masters can retrieve that flame either by going to the original soul or by directly retrieving a Spark from the Flame of God-Unity in the Heart of the Undifferentiated Source.

Once the Flame is reinstated in our hearts, we may be accelerated on our path of evolution to Enlightenment without the delay or distraction of finding our Twin Flame. The concept of such a reunion, however, still holds great attraction for each Twin Flame, in spite of its inherent difficulties. It is therefore stipulated in the plan of the Masters that bringing forth the Original Flame to each of the twins, can become, in and of itself, a force for the attraction of the Twin Flames to each other.

TEMPLATES AND BLUEPRINTS

For something, anything, to come into existence and take form, it first needs a set of energy imprints, or blueprints. These blueprints then cause that thing to manifest, in form, in our reality. To give you a crude example, I would assimilate a blueprint to the little chips on the surface of a circuit board, and the board itself as the template. The spiritual blueprints are energetic and etheric Light symbols which are held together inside an energetic template. These blueprints are held at various layers of reality in the Higher Realms where the records are kept.

When I am channeling and the Masters call forth the blueprint for something, I usually see them as small symbols encased in shiny Blue Lights shimmering down. I see them come spiraling down from the Heavens above. They look like the arrangements around the strands of DNA. They normally enter into the energy body of the person first, then move to lodge into the cell and DNA structure. When they enter the physical body, I normally see them enter the body from the top of the head at the Crown Chakra and spiral down to lodge themselves in specific parts. They may lodge into the DNA and cell structure of an organ, accumulate in a chakra, or form in the energy bodies or all the above. This Original Divine Blueprint, as its name implies, is the absolute most perfect and relevant design and plan for that thing. That perfect design was originally ordained in the Divine Plan. There always exists an Original Divine Blueprint, sometimes called the Perfected Blueprint for everything, absolutely everything, everyone and every place that has physical existence.

DIVINE PLAN

There is a plan, or a design, divinely ordained and crafted for everything which has manifest form. This plan is considered the Original Divine Plan. Some Great Being in the cosmos comes up with an idea or design, then that design is taken before a board, like the Karmic Board or a designated hierarchy of beings. The Hierarchy of Great Cosmic Beings in charge of creation would study and approve the plan. Then that plan would be perfectly designed, with every angle, every situation, every possible configuration crafted as an architect would design and craft a building. Then it would be handed over to the builders and specialists in every field to actually bring it into form. At any point in the process, if anything goes wrong or needs to be revised, everyone goes back to the Original Plan, the one that was Divinely Ordained.

The descriptions I have given here may seem to follow the same principles as life in our reality. Well, this is not surprising when you understand that our small and seemingly insignificant reality is only a microcosmic representation of the macrocosmic grand reality. The Masters continually remind me, *"As above, so below; as within, so without."*

On the other hand, if things were explained to us using other criteria than that which we ourselves use, we would not fully understand it anyway. We understand things of the other worldly realms when there is a point of reference to our realms and we can connect the dots to our own physical reality.

Have you ever wondered how a beautiful butterfly gets such amazing and intricate designs on its wings? Well, some Great Being was responsible for thinking out the Original Divine Plan for its existence and for designing that creature. Another approved it and yet another was given the task of building, or in this case, creating it. And we get to enjoy it. In this example the butterfly would represent the microcosmic perspective. To have an overall perspective, however, we would look at the issue of creation from a macrocosmic one.

A perfect example would be the creation of this Solar System and our Planet Earth. This I have explained in greater detail in the book, *Gifts from the Masters of Light: Journeys Into the Inner Realms of Consciousness — Gifts III.* I will present a brief synopsis of the story here, demonstrating the process of creation of the Divine Plan. A similar version is presented by Thomas Printz in *The Seven Mighty Elohim Speak on the Seven Steps Precipitation.*

Lord Helios and Lady Vesta, the deities of the sun, are considered to be the parents of our solar system. It is believed that they came up with the original idea for its creation. They took their idea to the Karmic Board for approval. Great Cosmic Beings such as Lord Melchior and Lady Melchai, the Galactic Logos in charge of our galaxy, the Milky Way, and Lord Melchizedek and Lady Malak, the Universal Logos, in charge of our universe as well as Lord Alpha and Lady Omega, our Cosmic Logos in charge of our entire Cosmic Conglomerate, sat on that board.

They voted on that idea and approved it. That idea was then turned into a Divine Plan. Time as we know it does not exist in these realms. However, from where we sit the plan took many millions of years to complete. That Original Divine Plan was made perfect in every way using elaborate blueprints for every aspect, every part and every detail. That perfect Original Plan was then bestowed upon a Great Cosmic Being known as the Great Silent Watcher. She took that Plan into her own heart and held the perfection of it in her mind for eons of time. Every species, every place, and every thing was reflected upon and held in her vision, and prayed over, allowing it to take form according to the perfection of the Original Divine Plan. From these reflections, the Original Template and the Divine Blueprints were formed. To bring that creation into manifest form, or rather to actually build the creation, piece by piece, the Elohim were called. Elohim are known to be the Architects of the Universe. They took the blueprints and replicated every detail in manifest form. The Angelic and Archangelic Forces of Light were brought in to guard each creation, species and thing or place. The Angelic Forces would be in charge of the macrocosmic aspects of things while the Elementals would be in charge of the microcosmic aspects. The Elementals are the small creatures commonly known in folklore as fairies and divas. Their job is to make sure every small unit in creation works in synch and perfect harmony with every other part.

Over eons of time, that is to say, over hundreds of thousands and possibly millions of years, the Original Blueprints became chipped, nicked and crooked and the Templates became faulty and scarred. This impacted both the Macrocosmic and Microcosmic levels represented in form and our bodies of matter. To reverse the damage and safeguard against further destruction, the Angelic Forces were given the task of restoring the Original Blueprints, healing our bodies, minds, emotions and even our souls. The Elementals were given the responsibility of healing and maintaining the cells, organs, and smaller, minute details of each creature, each place and each thing's existence. Both the Angelic Forces of Light and the Elementals are under the supervision of Metatron. Metatron, as the master-mind for the Original Perfect Divine Plan for absolutely all things in creation, knows both the macrocosmic and microcosmic perspectives.

Blueprint of the Divine Will

The very first blueprint ever fashioned was that of the Divine Will. After all, this entire planet and this solar system came about because of the Divine Ideas of Lord Helios and Lady Vesta and their Divine Will as the Solar Logos. To that was added the Divine Will of the Galactic Logos, the Universal Logos and the Cosmic Logos. The will of the Silent Watcher who held the Idea, the will of the Elohim who were the architects, the will of Great Cosmic Beings who brought the Original Seed of Life to Earth all play a role in this Divine Game.

That perfect Divine Blueprint was instilled in the beingness of all conscious souls. The souls who incarnated on Earth were affected by the density of the lower Earthly Realms. Humankind began to lose their alignment with the Divine Will. That is how Free Will was born. In *Path to Enlightenment, The Pillar of Light. Book I,* I have explained, in greater detail, the story of how we came to have Free Will. Suffice it to say, with our Free Will we began to wreak havoc in the fabric of Time and Space and cause disharmony and conflict in our lives. With this came greater immersion in chaos and further removal from the Divine Will.

To return to the Path of Light, to gain momentum in reaching Enlightenment, to live our Heaven on Earth, we need to re-establish the Divine Will and harmonize, or align our own personal will or Free Will with the Divine Will.

PERSONAL AND PLANETARY GRIDS

Thus far, I have mentioned ideas and designs, blueprints, and physically manifest objects. Let us look at the next stitch in the fabric of creation.

The journey of an idea from the realm of non-manifest to become an object manifested and active in our realm of reality, is a long and gradual process. There are various steps necessary for a creation to move from the realm of non-manifest, non-form, to the reality of manifest form and matter. First, there is an idea; the idea becomes a design; the design is set in motion and the motion becomes action. Through action the non-manifest becomes manifest. I have discussed the journey of the creation of our planet and our solar system from the design phase to the materially manifest phase. These are evolutionary phases and steps. For example, the next step in the evolutionary ladder for blueprints and templates is that they must be energetically "held in place". When a blueprint is embodied, it creates an energy signature. This becomes a matrix, or Grid of Light, within and around the object, person or place. If this Matrix is formed around a person, a creature or a thing, we call it a Personal Grid. There is a Personal Grid for every human, bird, animal, plant, rock, etc. This Personal Grid inherently connects to every other Personal Grid of that particular species and becomes part of that species' Grid. Therefore, every species, human, animal, etc. has a Grid.

A similar, much greater and more complex grid exists around the planet. This we call the Planetary Grid. The Planetary Grid is the Personal Grid for the Planet. It therefore contains each individual grid for every person, place or thing and the collective grid for every species. There is a Light which is illuminated on the Planetary Grid for every species, person, place or thing. The greater the number of a species, the more sparks of Light illuminate the Planetary Grid. This demonstrates the impact of the members of that species on the planet and its grid.

If there is only one member of a species alive on Earth, then that species will have its own Light Grid illuminated upon the Planetary Grid. Even extinct species still have their Grid displayed upon the Planetary Grid. However, their Light is dim. The importance of a Planetary and Personal Grid is that information can be shared and dispersed to the collective consciousness of a given species from any one member. Also, information can be dispersed from the Planetary Grid to Personal Grids and Species Grids.

The significance of this format is that the information can be shared and dispersed rapidly and each individual experience can benefit the collective consciousness of the species. The Hundredth Monkey Effect is a prime example of this process. When a certain body of knowledge is shared among the members of a specific species, their Personal Grids become active. When enough members of that species have their Personal Grids active, then critical mass is reached, and the collective Light begins to illuminate the Planetary Grid. At that point the Planetary Grid can actively transfer the information, data or event to all individuals of that species. Everyone is then able to benefit from the outcome. This adds to acceleration of the evolutionary process, preventing redundancies.

LIGHT GRIDS AND CANDLE GRIDS

A Light Grid is a matrix of Light which is specifically created to induce a desired outcome. For example, when Metatron or Goddess Hecate gives us a Grid of Light formation or a candle grid exercise, they induce a specific controlled outcome or objective. This objective may be to relieve us from karma and karmic entanglement, bring healing to our bodies, help accelerate us or intercede on our behalf to alter the course of events for a better outcome in alignment with our Divine Mission. The mechanism that the Grid of Light uses to achieve the desired outcome is to post a specific intention upon our Personal Grid. They then accelerate that intention or magnify its impact by asking other Great Beings, such as angels and other Masters, to constantly shine their Light upon us.

The beauty of a Light Grid Formation is that it can become the accumulated force, power of intention and intercession of many beings.

For example, when you stand in the center of a circle, triangle, square or any other sacred geometry in the company of Masters, Angelic Forces and Thrones, you are blessed by the magnitude of the power of those Beings. Combine this with the power of the Light Beams and Rays which are brought forth, together with dispensations, invocations, decrees, mantras, prayers and you increase and magnify the impact exponentially.

Candle grids are an example of the magnification potential of the Five Elements used to our advantage. The Five Elements are the building blocks of our creation. Everything in our manifest creation has come about from the combined forces of some or all of the Elements – Earth, Water, Fire, Air and Ether. Four are considered base elements and the fifth, Ether, is a sublime element. The four base elements are held within Ether.

A candle grid has alchemical potencies. When lit, it summons all the elements to itself. The candle wax represents both the Water and Earth elements. The flame represents the Fire element and requires Air to burn. Thus all Elements are present and actively involved. Lighting candles in intentional candle grid and Light Grid formations can have potent powers. Intentions, together with the alchemical qualities of lighted candles, imbued with the presence of Great Beings, can alter the course of events to our advantage.

To further increase the potency, some candle grids incorporate crystals. These are called Magnification Grids. The crystals magnify the potencies of the candles and the intentions set to be achieved. They also clear the energy from around the grid environment and add potency to the emanations of Light to help anchor the intent.

RELEASING PAIN AND STRUGGLE

All negative energies, all lower vibrational forces, all pain, all struggles, all traumas, all conflict and all negative emotions will have to come to the surface and be released before we can reach Enlightenment. As Metatron says, *"We must first empty the cup from its poison before we can fill it with nectar."* The negative, dark and painful energies we have endured for many lifetimes as well as those spread upon the atmosphere and environment of Earth and the Five Elements must come to the surface to be released. *"Coming to the surface"* can happen in many ways and through many layers. For example we, as individuals, release our dross, our collective consciousness as a species releases its dross and the planet releases her dross. All layers must participate in emptying their individual and collective cups. The Masters give us guidance and direction to assist us in understanding what needs to be released and how to accomplish it on behalf of the planet, the collective consciousness of all souls and ourselves. As we empty our cups, we become the pioneers and spearheads to help the multitudes and masses do the same.

We release layers from our physical body, emotional body, mental body, and spiritual body. The same applies to us collectively as a species and to Earth as a planetary body. When we begin to "spring-clean" our bodies, the impact can bring to the surface the conflictive energies held within our bodies, minds and emotions. Physical sickness, especially flu symptoms are common examples. When Earth releases her dross and spring-cleans, the impact shows up as floods, cyclones, hurricanes, earthquakes, volcanic eruptions, tsunamis and such.

Karma and Karmic Entanglement

A re-occurring theme in this book, as well as in Book I, is the release of karma and karmic entanglement. If you are beginning to wonder how many ways there are to release karma and how much karma is there to be released, the answer is as many ways as you choose to and as much of it as you choose to release. There is karma or actions for every day that we live and every lifetime which we have experienced in physical embodiment. For as long as we come back to the body, we incur karma. Karma literally means actions in Sanskrit. Everyone, everything, every place which exists in the manifest world is subject to karma or action and for every action, there is a reaction. That is a law of physics, as a scientist would say or that is a physical law, as the Masters would say.

The Law of Karma, or Cause and Effect, is a physical as well as a spiritual law that we are bound to, for as long as we live on Earth. That is to say, for as long as we choose to be bound by it while we live on Earth. There are indeed other superior laws which we could choose to live by. However, that would only happen if and when we can reach levels of Light where we can dissolve all karma and leave it behind. At that point, we could live with and abide by the Universal Law of Divine Love.

Even the Living Masters and Ascended Masters are bound by the Law of Cause and Effect, or by Karma. How so? Because we drag them into it. For as long as a being is born into physicality, even if they are Masters and Avatars, they are affected by the karma they take on our behalf. Living Masters are bound by us and our karma. They are here to physically remove it with their Light. Ascended Masters are not physically bound, yet for as long as they are in our service, most of their time is spent helping us out of our karmic misery. They continue to put every effort into teaching us how to relieve ourselves of its grip. Therefore, if you continue to read about release of karma and karmic entanglement, best assume that it is for your own good and for the good of all your loved ones, including the Masters whom I hope have joined the entourage of those you love.

FREE WILL AND KARMIC ENTANGLEMENT

Life on planet Earth is based on Free Will. This means that human beings have a right to will themselves in or out of any situation at any time. Even though you may feel stuck in some situations, with your Free Will you can move on at any time. However, it is best to move on when you have released your karmic entanglements and have closure because when you quit, when you can no longer take it anymore and decide to move on, you will be taking the entire karmic situation and deferring it to another round in this lifetime or other lifetimes. It is best, therefore, to deal with karmic issues at the first go-around, in this lifetime if possible and not postpone it to another lifetime. It takes less effort and energy to complete something once and for all, than to come back and do it all over again. It is also better to learn the lessons the first time around and not differ to second and third rounds. However, as we all know, this too is easier said than done.

THRONES OF GOD

Through the pages of these books you will be called to visit various Thrones. These Thrones are the abode or seat of that Universal Consciousness we call God, Great Spirit, or other names. In Book I, the focus was on fully experiencing the energies of the Throne of the I Am That I Am and the I Am Presence. This is an aspect of that Universal Consciousness which is most immersed in these realms of matter and form. It is therefore the one which is closest to us. We know it as God in Form. The individual self, separate and isolated from Oneness, will need to know this aspect of God and merge into its energies in order to find solace and union.

Imagine moving through a spectrum of Light and a hierarchy of existence with one hundred and forty-four layers. These one hundred and forty-four layers are also called dimensions of realities. Whether there are an exact number of dimensions related to each of these is beyond my comprehension. What helps me understand the process is to envision them as realms of reality. Manifest form evolves from solid matter form to ethereal form, to semi-form, to non-form, to Pure Energy, to Pure Light, to Pure Creation and finally to Pure Silence.

In the third dimension of reality, we experience the densest and most solid aspect of this spectrum and at the top, in the one hundred forty-fourth dimension of reality, we are told by the Masters that there is no matter. There are landmark points along the levels, where we are brought before Thrones upon which an aspect of God is the presiding deity. It has taken me the course of over two decades to be brought before each individual throne which I have been invited to. It is my understanding that, as we grow in the course of our spiritual evolution, we attain the merit to be brought before a greater aspect of God residing at a higher Throne. This is most generally the case although there have been times when I have been brought to a Throne and its residing deity which fits somewhere between two I had visited before. The exact sequence of the Hierarchy of Thrones was not given to me all at once; nor was I aware that these Thrones were indeed related to aspects of God. The suggestion that God would have many aspects, who are residing upon various Thrones, seemed redundant until I understood that one can only earn the merit to be brought to the next higher Throne when one's Quotient of Light increases to a certain appointed level.

At that point I became belligerent and demanded to be brought before the highest God there ever was. I threatened that I would stop meditating if this demand was not immediately met. Better still, I said, I would not stop meditating until I am brought before the ultimate, utmost high God there ever was. I would not eat nor sleep but meditate constantly in order to put my petition forth. I claimed that this was a preposterous system, and the proof was our plight, misery and pain of living in this terrible world. This, I lamented, was happening to us because a lower God, someone who does not know what they are doing, is in charge of our world. To recount the entire story, although humorous, is beyond the scope of this book, suffice it to say that this meditation strike was challenged when I was given an analogy, a parable, to contend with and I was left to resolve the issue on my own. From their point of view, I suppose, I was the unruly child who needed a good talking to and left alone to snap out of it in my own time. The parable was, *"If a nail falls off your finger where would you return it to?"* The moral of the parable was that if you returned the nail to the head, even though the command center of the body, it would not have any use for it. The nail is useful to the finger, from which it came and to which it needs to return.

At the time of that event I was the equivalent of the nail and my God, or my Guardian was the finger. When, as a nail, I could become aware of my place in the scheme of things and understand my relationship to the finger, then I would be ready to be introduced to the hand, then the arm, then other parts of the body, the head and finally the whole body. Our relationship with God is somewhat similar to this parable. The Great God, Universal Consciousness of All That Is, would be like the entire body in this analogy. While we, as the nail, are not aware of our place on the body, we would not appreciate or understand our place in the great plan nor would we know the role of the whole. That understanding came for me much later and even then, I could not be reverent about it. I maintained that you have to go to the top if you want to get anything done right, in the first place. I of course, am a product of the duality which believes that if a lower aspect of God, e.g. the finger is in charge of me, the higher aspect of God, e.g. the whole body would not be involved in the matter. I was unable to see that the whole is always involved in all matters, yet it was in my best interest to start building a personal relationship with all the parts in order to appreciate and understand the whole. Neal Donald Walsh, the author of *Conversations with God, book I–III* recounts a similar experience, where God tells him that there is another God beyond the one who is communicating with him. He gives a witty and humorous accounting of his displeasure from this disclosure.

Why then, you might ask, am I trying to spoon feed you, or even force feed you this information, fast and furious, if that is indeed the case. The answer is; I did it the hard way over two decades so that you can do it the easy way over the course of reading these books. I can give you a framework, yet neither I nor anyone else can make it happen for you. The experience is yours to have, if and when you truly choose to have it for yourself. My job is to map out the teachings and my experiences, with the help of the Masters. I am here to give you pointers. What you do with it is your Free Will choice. The fact that you have come so far as reading this book tells me, and hopefully you, that you are ready.

It is a Universal Law that if one member of a species has an experience, goes through an evolutionary shift or makes a ground breaking discovery, that experience, that shift, that discovery is available for every member of that species to benefit from or to pay the price for. In this case, I pray that we all benefit. You may say that I have gone through experiences categorically known as esoteric, metaphysical, supernatural and such, in order to bring them out of the realm of the unknown to the known and map them for your benefit. By doing so, I was given the merit to personalize the experience. This means that the sum total of it is now posted in my Personal Light Grid or the Matrix of Light which holds me together. Mapping it out and anchoring it in my Personal Grid means that it is now posted on the Planetary Grid for use by every member of our species.

To help you with a mental picture of the Hierarchy of Thrones, I will briefly present those relevant to this book. The main focus of this book is to fully embody and anchor the energies of the Throne of YHWH. The focus of Book I was to do the same with the Throne of the I Am That I Am and the I Am Presence, God in Form. The following are Thrones we will briefly visit in this book and work with more extensively in future books in this series.

UNDIFFERENTIATED SOURCE

The Source, in non-form or non-manifest, is Undifferentiated Source. This is the Source of the Universal Consciousness wherein resides all creation in non-manifest or undifferentiated form. The Throne of Undifferentiated Source resides in the one hundred and eighth realm of reality. The deity which resides upon this Throne is simply Pure White Light. When I go to this abode, I see myself enter a space filled with Light. While there, I am filled with this Light and experience lightness within me. You can say my body too, becomes Pure Light or that I was conscious of having a body. Then I start ascending upward, moving into a dense but Pure White Light Energy. I am at this point filled with complete bliss.

From here on, the concept of form is only an idea; a mental precept which the mind is reluctant to fully conceive of, or embrace. I hear direction and guidance issued to me, with enormous love from the being of this Throne. I must add that it took me more than a year from the time when I was introduced to the concept of Undifferentiated Source to when I was allowed to enter into this realm and to the time when I could actually hear guidance. Around the end of that time, I was given the understanding that there exists a Throne above this one whose Light illumines the Undifferentiated Source. For more on this and the dimensional layers, read Brian Grattan's *The Mahatma I and II.*

PARAMATMAN LIGHT

This is a Throne of God which resides in the one hundred and twenty-second realm of reality. Paramatman denotes the state beyond individualization. Paramatman is a Sanskrit word which denotes Para and Atman. Where Atman is the Self, Paramatman is the Supreme Self. Imagine the ocean of Oneness as Paramatman. Atman is a drop from that ocean of Oneness; a drop who remembers its true origin. We forget that our own individualized self, is Atman and our Supreme Self is Para-matman, when we live in this density. The knowledge of the Self as a united essence forever in Oneness with All, is lost. The harshness of this dense world and the immense energetic pollution are the cause of our inability to connect to our Self and our Supreme Self. The Throne of Paramatman resides above the Throne of Undifferentiated Source. The Paramatman Light is the Light which illuminates the Throne of Undifferentiated Source.

THE THRONE OF ABSOLUTE

Divine Mother resides upon the Throne of Absolute, at the hundred and twenty-second realm of reality. Even though this Throne is in the deep core of non-manifest realms, I do have impressions of form when I am brought to this Throne. I see Divine Mother seated at her Throne upon a raised platform. The seats of the Seven Lords of Light and the Maha Lord of Light are arranged in a crescent moon shape in front of her Throne, on a lower platform. There are other realms of reality which stretch beyond this Throne, over which Divine Mother also has dominion. One is the Throne of Creation, the abode of the Pool of Creation. Another is the Throne of Feminine Principle, the abode of the Pure Energy vibration of the Feminine Creative Force, which is the Mother Force for Creation in all realms.

In *Path to Enlightenment, Books III and IV*, we will explore these Thrones more extensively as many of the Chapters merit such excursions. The full hierarchy of the Thrones, as it has been given to me so far, will be discussed. I have not as yet come across any printed materials where the hierarchies of the Thrones have been mentioned in similar format to which I present. It is however, possible that such material exists or that it will be brought forth by others in time to come. It is my belief that if there is truth in any material, it will uphold its value and ring true for all at some point. It is also my belief that all truths must be spoken and heard before they can be upheld.

THE SEVEN RAYS

White Light on its journey down to the realms of form begins to contact physical matter. This contact causes the White Light to become differentiated or fractured, just as sunlight shining through a prism is split or fractured. From this event, Seven Rays are created. You see the Seven Rays illuminated in nature as a rainbow, a sun-bow or a moon-bow. Whenever Pure Light faces resistance, it fractures into fragments. Those fragments are the Rays. These Seven Rays become the catalyst to uphold a specific energy and quality brought forth from the higher realms. Energies and qualities of the Seven Rays are, from One to Seven, Divine Love, Divine Wisdom, Divine Power, Focus and Concentration, Truth and Healing, Service, Transmutation and Order. The Beams of Light emanating from each of the Seven Rays bring the focus of that Divine Quality into this third dimensional realm. The lower dimensional realms are then charged with these Seven Rays, the differentiated version of the Pure White Light. In the Higher

Dimensional Realms, the Light remains Pure and Brilliant and therefore, undifferentiated as Pure White Light. Undifferentiated Source is the source of "All That Is" before the Light separated or multiplied itself into Seven Rays and into form. The Seven Rays of Light in their descent into density move through the Thrones and ultimately reach into the solidified bodies of matter.

Each individual human being, incarnate on Earth at this present time, is therefore, illuminated or has become enlivened by the emanations from one of the Seven Rays. The Ray remains the same for each individual and all souls in that soul lineage i.e. souls from the First Ray, Second Ray, etc. (for more on the Seven Rays, refer to *The Lords of the Seven Rays*, by Mark and Elizabeth Clare Prophet and *Gifts III*, by Nasrin Safai).

The souls for each Ray have a cycle of time to incarnate on Earth, learn their lessons and leave to make room for the souls of the next Ray. That was the intention written into the Original Divine Plan for this phase of Earth's evolution. However, at this present moment, the Earth is over polluted and over populated because the souls from all the Rays, One through Seven, are still here. We need to open ourselves to receive much greater Light from the Undifferentiated Source and the Paramatman Light. This will raise the vibration of Earth and all souls, helping them to find their way to greater Light and leave these lower vibrational frequencies where pain and struggle reign. The ideal solution would be to bring the Light and immerse these lower dimensions into the Seven Rays, thereby relieving Earth and the souls of their pollution. Once cleansed, their vibration can be raised to Higher Light, to Brilliant Light, to Pure White Light. This is why Metatron calls upon the Light from Paramatman and the Heart-core of the Undifferentiated

Source to pour down. He calls forth this Light to the I Am That I Am and through it to the bodies of all souls. We have the choice to accelerate our spiritual growth by receiving this Light, embodying this Light and becoming this Light. Then we will become the conduit for dispensing the Light to all souls and to Earth.

In the course of this book, other Rays are mentioned. These are Beams of Light with special qualities other than the Seven Rays, brought to Earth by the Masters, to assist in the anchoring of the Seven Rays and the establishment of those qualities.

FRAMEWORK

Archangel Michael is the Angel of Mercy and the protector of humankind from darkness. As such, he is the Savior or rescuer of all souls from the bondage of enslavement to Earth, to the body, and to Earthly needs and bodily desires. In Chapter I, Archangel Michael, speaks of the Twin Flames and the Flame of God-Unity. By re-establishing the energy of Twin Flames and uniting the Twins from an energetic standpoint, we will be able to fully ignite the Flame of God-Unity within our own Heart Chakras. This is the true experience of Oneness; it will cause the release of duality, separation, and fears resulting from the original splitting of a soul into two halves and the separation of each half from the other. Furthermore, the Template of Joy is called by Archangel Michael to seal the over-laying of the Flame of God-Unity to each individual.

In Chapter II, Master Jesus offers to reinstate the Template of Divine Will by calling its blueprint to form inside our Heart Chakras, while we stand at the Throne of the I Am That I Am, God in Form. To accelerate us, Master Jesus accompanies us on a journey to the next throne, the Throne of YHWH. Here, twenty-four Elders are seated around the Throne. They hold the vibration of Divine Will singing the sacred mantra, *"Holy, Holy, Holy is the Lord, God of Hosts."* Four creatures with faces resembling a horse, an ox, an eagle and a lion stand at the four corners of the Throne. They are the Guardians of the Secrets of the Heavenly Realms and the Keepers of Light. We return from this journey with the Template of Divine Will safely embedded in our Heart Chakras.

In Chapter III, Goddess Hecate, the Goddess of Power and Passion, offers us a candle grid. This grid is designed to magnify the transmutational powers of the Purple Ray and Golden Ray to clear the emotional body and the mental body through the use of purple and gold candles. When the mind is clear and the emotions are pure, we are empowered.

In Chapter IV, St. Germain guides us to release negativity and fear. He reminds us that to reach Enlightenment we need to relinquish all darkness. This he helps us do by bringing us before the Thrones of I Am That I Am, YHWH and Undifferentiated Source. On our behalf, he requests the release of negativity and the return of the guardianship of the Lords of Light. Finally, he offers us his own guiding Light as the Master or Cohan of the Seventh Ray, whose age (the Seventh Golden Age) is approaching. He also reminds us that he has been appointed as the Maha Cohan of the next 98,000 year cycle of Light which begins after the Seventh Golden Age is complete. A Maha Cohan plays a supervisory role to all the Seven Cohan of the Seven Rays. The next grand cycle of 98,000 years will begin in another 14,000 years when the Seventh Golden Age is complete and St. Germain, as the Maha Cohan will preside over the entire grand cycle. We can call upon his intercession both as the Cohan of this cycle and also as the Maha Cohan of the next grand cycle.

In Chapter V, Metatron speaks about the return of peace and harmony to Earth as the outcome of a phase of spring-cleaning. Once we release anger, greed, deception, fear and pain, we can make room for truth, peace, harmony and joy. Metatron offers insight of the Global impact of energies coming from the sun for the release of dross from our planet. He then speaks of the return of energies of Truth to replace the dross.

In Chapter VI, Metatron offers us exercises in releasing karmic entanglements. He gives an invocational mantra with a most loving energy to help us forgive and heal the scars of unhappy relationships. By repeating this exercise, we can allow ourselves to heal the pain, forgiving ourselves and others and moving on with our lives.

In Chapter VII, Metatron offers us a clearing and healing exercise by bringing up the Red Life Force Energy from Earth and the Pure White Light from the Heavens and mixing it in our bodies. From the mixing, the Rose-Pink Healing Light of Heaven and Earth fills our bodies. This Rose-Pink Light is capable of instilling within us the love which binds this entire Universe together. When we walk the Earth aware and connected to this loving force, life can become pleasant and joyful, our endeavors in serving the Earth and all souls, a blessing.

In Chapter VIII, Metatron gives us a prayer to invoke the Light of Paramatman to pour down upon us from the realms beyond where Undifferentiated Source resides. This is the realm where Light is bright and pure. The Throne of Undifferentiated Source is the abode of God in non-manifest or Undifferentiated Light. Paramatman is the Light which pours upon this Throne to energize and embody this Throne. Through the invocational decree presented in this chapter, we call upon the Light of Paramatman and the Throne of Undifferentiated Source to actively over-light and embody us. Imbued with this Light, we become powerful beacons of Light to raise the vibrational frequency of Earth and influence the process of awakening all souls to their Divinity.

In Chapter IX, Metatron offers us an Alchemical Grid of Light to address three important issues; healing, protection and manifestation. As mentioned in the first part of this Introduction, we begin by healing ourselves from the pain and dross in order to gain greater Light. We then protect the Light and maintain it at a high vibrational frequency; this will then promote the manifestation of a better life for ourselves and others in this mundane realm. This exercise combines all three steps into one Grid of Light calling upon the Healing Light of Mother Mary, the Protective Light of Quan Yin, and the combined healing and protection of the Angelic Forces of Light and Metatron, to manifest greater acceleration of our growth. Metatron gives us an idea of the level of acceleration available through this exercise using the analogy of the microwave oven compared to a conventional oven.

In Chapter X, Metatron calls upon the Seven Lords of Light, the Guardians of all Light for our entire planet. The object of this exercise is to clear our Five Body System of dross and fill us with the nectar of love from the Creative Pool of the Feminine Principle. Metatron states,

"To bring the spirit of the Creative Force to all bodies of matter on Earth, you can begin to work with different aspects of the Divine Mother, the Feminine Principle of Creation. For example, Goddess Athena's wisdom and essence as a Warrior Goddess is sorely needed at this present juncture in Earth's evolution. We are also in need of the Goddess of Victory and Goddess of Liberty. Goddess of Victory has been victorious for over 200,000 years, Goddess of Liberty has been liberating humankind from the dross of fear for over 500,000 years and Goddess Athena has been the Warrior Goddess of all women, all soldiers and all teachers for a few thousand years."

It is therefore appropriate to offer you this Grid of Light with Goddess Athena, Goddess of Victory and Goddess of Liberty. This Grid brings forth some of the highest and most potent Feminine aspects to us and to Earth.

In Chapter XI, Metatron brings forth a Grid of Light to release negative energies and lower vibrational forces from our bodies and the body of the planet. The point of this Grid is to release the extra dross we pick up from the planet while she is freeing herself from her own pain, struggle and dross of eons of time of emersion in lower vibration. As beacons of Light, we are able to help free her from these lower frequencies and raise the vibration of Earth and all humankind. In the process, we continuously pick up more than our bodies, minds, emotions and souls are able to manage at any given time. By calling forth such Great Cosmic Beings as the Great Silent Watcher and the Angelic Forces of the Four Directions, Metatron sets out to clear and cleanse our energy bodies and that of the planet. A beautiful invocational mantra, calling upon various transmutational and healing Light Rays, makes this exercise potent and long-lasting.

In Chapter XII, Divine Mother offers a discourse on seeking abundance, prosperity and Divine Intervention through her and aspects of her which we know as Goddesses and Female Deities. Goddess Hecate brings forth an Abundance Magnification Candle Grid to catapult our growth and acceleration in both the sublime and mundane realms. She calls upon thirteen aspects of the Divine Mother to add their own special qualities to the candle grid. Both Divine Mother and Metatron insist on the understanding that, in today's world, poverty is not a requirement for attaining spirituality. In fact, for as long as we struggle for survival, we miss the chance to serve. When part, most, or all our energy is spent providing for our basic needs, i.e. the survival needs of the body, we cannot fully function as spiritually evolved beings. We are spiritually empowered when the struggle for survival has ceased to hold us in its grip. When we can leave survival issues behind and reach the point where we not only provide for our own needs but also for the needs of the multitudes and masses, we can rightfully claim that we are "in the world and not of it". Then, what we are and what we have is dedicated and devoted in the service of Light and the multitudes and masses.

This abundance grid was given to me in January of 2008 to accelerate the work of FAGU, the Foundation for the Attainment of God-Unity, and to encapsulate the power and might necessary to bring to publication the books in the Path to Enlightenment series. I kept this grid going every day until August when we began to finalize the last drafts of the four initial books in the series. At that point, She allowed me to share this Abundance Grid in the August 2008 Newsletter on my website. This triggered a series of abundance grids offered to us by Metatron and other Masters who joined forces with Divine Mother to accelerate the abundance manifestation process. These I will share with you in Book III and IV of the *Path to Enlightenment* series.

A GUIDE TO THE CHAKRAS
OF THE PHYSICAL BODY AND THEIR LOCATIONS

Chakras are energy centers that are located upon a central column along the spine. Most traditional thinking refers to seven chakras which are located in the body. In order from lowest to highest, they are: the Root, Sacral Plexus, Solar Plexus, Heart, Throat, Third Eye, and Crown. There are chakras below the Root Chakra which connect us to Earth, and chakras above the Crown Chakra which connect us to the Higher Realms and Heavens above.

Although not traditionally mentioned, there are two other energy centers in the body which the Masters have taught us in our channeling sessions. These are called the Seat of the Soul and the Cosmic Heart. The Seat of the Soul energy center, or chakra, is located halfway between the Heart Chakra and the Solar Plexus, just below the rib cage. The Cosmic Heart Chakra or energy center is located high on your chest, midway between the Heart Chakra and the Throat Chakra. The Cosmic Heart Chakra sits over the thymus gland. We continue to refer to the traditional system of seven chakras and do not allocate a number for the Cosmic Heart and Seat of the Soul Chakras, yet we place equal importance on them.

The chakras of the body above the Crown extend all the way to the thirteenth dimension of reality. The Throne of the I Am That I Am resides in this dimension. The Perfected Presence of the I Am, God in Form, sits upon this Throne. This is considered our Twelfth Chakra.

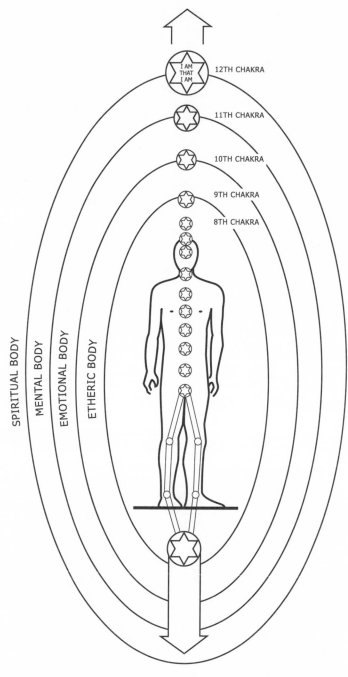

12TH CHAKRA

11TH CHAKRA

10TH CHAKRA

9TH CHAKRA

8TH CHAKRA

I AM
THAT
I AM

SPIRITUAL BODY

MENTAL BODY

EMOTIONAL BODY

ETHERIC BODY

THE FIVE BODY SYSTEM

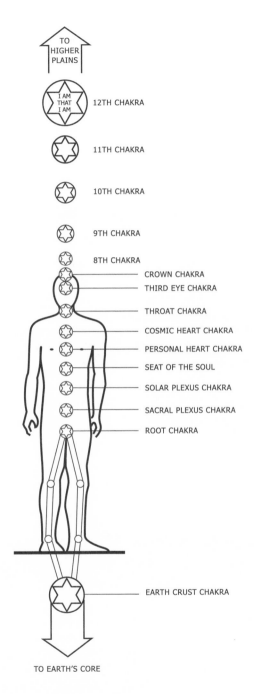

THE CHAKRA SYSTEM

CHAPTER STRUCTURE

Each chapter begins with an introduction given by me, Nasrin. Then the channeled material begins with each Master identifying themselves with their own special style of greeting. For example, Metatron always begins with *"Beloveds of my own heart, I am Metatron, take a deep breath with me."* Archangel Michael always greets us with *"My Brethren of Light, I am Michael,"* Jesus always begins with, *"Adonai Beloveds, I am Jeshua Ben Joseph,"* and Goddess Hecate and Quan Yin always address us by saying, *"My Children of Light, I am Goddess Hecate or Quan Yin."*

The channeled material also ends when the Master closes with his or her own special signature closing. This usually occurs at the end of each chapter.

Please note these important points in order to distinguish between my introduction and the channeled material.

CHAPTER I

RELEASE BETRAYAL AND RESTORE GOD-UNITY

We begin the first chapter and the first month of the year with a profound exercise which encapsulates healing, release and acceleration on the path to Enlightenment, immersed in the joy of union. In this exercise, Archangel Michael calls upon the original template of Divine Mission to re-establish us in Oneness with our Source. Aspects of personality and fragments of soul are called forth in this meditation to reside in peace, harmony and Oneness with one another within us. Fears of bondage, enslavement and karmic debt are released. The Template of Joy is called to replace everything which was released.

Archangel Michael also calls the Original Blueprint for the energies of Twin Flames. By re-establishing the energy of Twin Flames in the Cosmic Heart Chakra and uniting the Twins energetically, he ignites the Flame of God-Unity within our hearts.

My Brethren of Light, I Am Michael.

I have been the Angel of Protection and your Guardian for eons of time. I stand with my Sword of Mercy held above your head to protect you from all harm. I ask you to come to me in times of need. I ask of you to wrap yourself in the Mantle of Blue Light from Archangel Michael everyday as you awaken. Call upon me and ask for the Mantle of Blue Light to engulf you. Feel the presence of the Mantle wrap itself like a cocoon around your physical body and all your energy bodies. The moment you begin to feel protection from the Mantle of Blue Light, you will know that you will no longer be in harm's way. Negative energies sent to you through people's words, thoughts or actions will not affect you. Such negativity will not reach to your physical body or energy bodies because when it comes into contact with the Mantle, it is dissolved without penetration. Begin your day by calling forth Archangel Michael and say,

"Archangel Michael above me, Archangel Michael below me, Archangel Michael in front of me, Archangel Michael behind me, Archangel Michael to my left, Archangel Michael to my right, Archangel Michael around me, Archangel Michael within me, Archangel Michael spread the Mantle of Blue Light all around me and encapsulate me like a cocoon. Archangel Michael blaze forth the Light, blaze forth the Light, blaze forth the Light." Say this and feel the protection around you.

I will now call upon my Legions of Light, Protection and Mercy, the Legions of Michael. I also call upon Lady Faith, who is my own Twin Flame or consort, and her Legions. I ask Lady Faith to stand with her Sword of Faith held above you. I stand with my Sword of Mercy above your head. I ask now for the Template of Joy to be released from the Presence of the I Am That I Am down into your physical and energy bodies. The Template will move through all the levels and layers, to the thirteenth dimension and further down to the third dimension of reality. It will move through a Pillar of Light which we will establish around you. Take a deep breath and prepare to receive the Pillar of Light with the Template of Joy inside.

Visualize a Pillar of Light extending down to you. Inside of the Pillar of Light, the energies of God in Form are descending in Pure White Light. This Pillar will descend and engulf you. Around this Pillar, the Legions of Lady Faith stand in a circle. Faith is standing in front of you with her Sword of Faith held above your head. Around the circle of Faith stands the Legions of Michael with their Swords of Mercy drawn out. I stand behind you with my Sword of Mercy touching the point of the Sword of Lady Faith. From the contact between the point of my Sword and Lady Faith's Sword, a Blue and Pink Light begins to stream down cocooning you. Take a deep breath.

We call forth the Template of Joy to be downloaded and established in your Throat Chakra, Cosmic Heart Chakra, Personal Heart Chakra, Solar Plexus Chakra, Sacral Plexus Chakra and your Root Chakra. From this point on you may speak your truth without fear and live life in surrender. Take a deep breath.

We ask for the release of all the energies of betrayal, rejection and abandonment from the entire cell structure, the DNA structure, the personality aspects and the soul aspects. We ask for the Spirit to be freed from all entanglements; physical, karmic and etheric. All dross accumulated from many lifetimes of struggle and pain around you and within you is now released.

I call forth, in the name of the I Am That I Am, the release of the energies of bondage and enslavement from all lifetimes. All karma and bondage to another soul and to your own soul or personality aspects is to be released now. All cords of negative energy created by you or by any other person, place or thing, group, event or circumstance is now released. You are now free from all karmic entanglements of this lifetime, past lifetimes, future lifetimes. Say,

"I ask for the release of all events, circumstances, people, places and things from my physical body, my etheric body, my emotional body, my mental body, and my spiritual body which no longer serve my highest good. I release it through all levels and layers of my Five Body System from my past, present and future; in all dimensions of reality, in all time and in no time. I ask for the release of all fear of debt, bondage and enslavement from all aspects of my personalities and all aspects of my soul. I now ask for the return of trust, acceptance and surrender to my Higher Self. I reside and live my life from this point on knowing that I Am One with God; God's Light shines within me and through me to others. I now call forth the Template of my Divine Mission to be downloaded to me. I ask for my energetic and etheric connection with my Twin Flame to be restored. I ask for this healing on my own behalf and on behalf of my Twin Flame. I call upon the Higher Self of my Twin Flame wherever he/she may be, in physical embodiment or non-physical realms. I ask for the fire that illuminates and brings forth God-Unity to now begin to shine in the personal Hearts and in the Cosmic Hearts of my Twin Flame and myself. I ask Archangel Michael to intercede on behalf of all humankind and all individuals who wish to receive this flame. I call forth the Flame of God-Unity to be established in my Cosmic Heart. I ask this flame to begin to illuminate the Cosmic Heart and personal Hearts of my Twin Flame and myself. I fully acknowledge this to be the union of Twin Flames, leading to the experience of Oneness. I ask that every individual may feel the wholeness resulting from this union within themselves, whether they have the chance to meet their Twin Flame in this lifetime or not."

Take a deep breath and pause to allow the Template to be established in your Five Body System.

Once the energies of the Twin Flames are united, you do not need the physical presence of your Twin Flame to experience Unity. Ideally, the ultimate experience of Unity can be attained when the Twins find each other. However, so few Twins have the chance to find each other at this point of their evolution that we now have to resort to the establishment of the actual Flame of the Twins in the Heart as a symbol of that union and to request for the Flame of God-Unity to fully embody and over-light it. This will accelerate all stages and phases of growth to promote the final phase of Enlightenment. By re-establishing the energy of Twin Flames in the Heart and uniting the Twins from an energetic standpoint, you will be able to energize the Flame of God-Unity within your own Hearts. We, therefore, ask for the dispensation to ignite the Fire of the Twin Flames in your Heart. Through the course of the next three months the Twin Flames are to become fully active and operational.

The Flame of God-Unity leads you to the final goal of union; the true experience of Oneness. It will release duality and separation. It will free you from fears resulting from the original splitting of your soul into two halves and the separation of each half from the other. Karma and karmic entanglements will be cleared out. People who instilled fear within you, those who inflicted pain upon you and places and things which have filled you with memories of fearful events, will no longer grip you in their hold or trap you in their energy field. Take a deep breath.

TEMPLATE OF FREEDOM FROM BONDAGE

I now call forth the Template of Freedom from Bondage to be downloaded into your body. All traces of enslavement, bondage, betrayal and separation are now removed. I now call forth the Template for the return to God-Unity to be installed upon your Five Body System. Every cell, molecule and iota of your being is now imbued with the Light from the Flame of God-Unity. The energies move through the Presence of the I Am That I Am into your body.

This Template I now activate in the name of the I Am That I Am, in the name of the Twin Flames, in the name of the Flame of God-Unity, the Eternal Flame. This template is the Divine Right of every human being. It is now activated in the space of your Cosmic Heart. It will extend and expand to reach your personal Heart Chakra and to illumine your individual Heart. It will reconnect the individual small self to the Great Self or God Self. I now call forth the wisdom of the ages to be downloaded to you from the God-Source, so that you may benefit from the Source of All Wisdom and All Knowledge.

The Creator Source is now allowing you to connect to the Universal Mind and benefit from the Great Pool of Wisdom. You are now able to establish a relationship with and pave a pathway to access the wisdom available from the Mind of God. You are no longer limited. You will not act from fear or from the karma of your past. Divine intervention is brought to you from the mind of the Creator-God. This Divine intervention will clear all karmic entanglements and free you from bondage. It will hold you hostage to no one, no thing, no space, and no time. Take a deep breath.

TEMPLATE OF DIVINE UNION

I now call forth the Template of Divine Union, the union of the small-self, the ego-self, with the God Self, the Divine Self. I ask in the name of the I Am That I Am and in the name of YHWH for the complete merging of the small self into the Great Self. I ask for this Template to continue to download and to reach higher levels of merging, day by day, for the next three months and beyond, until complete.

I hold my Sword of Mercy drawn out of its sheath to protect and to guard you on your path to greater Light. In you I place my hope, my Light and my love.

I am your brother Michael. So it is.

"I offer you my Will in total surrender.
I ask that my Will be aligned with your Will.
Not my Will but Thy Will be done."
Jeshua Ben Joseph

CHAPTER II

THE GOLDEN THRONE

December, preceding each New Year, sets the pace for entry into the Gregorian calendar year, used by the Western World but February sets the pace for Earth's natural cycle, which begins at March Equinox (March 20-22).

Master Jesus takes us before the Throne of I Am That I Am in the thirteenth dimension to receive the Blueprint of Divine Will. He then takes us further out in the realms of Light to visit the Throne of YHWH in the twenty-second dimension of reality. On our return journey, Master Jesus invokes the essence of I Am That I Am to accompany us and to sit inside the Lotus of the Crown on top of our heads. This lotus resides on top of every human being's head. At first it sits on top of the head as a bud. As we grow spiritually, the lotus begins to open up. When fully open it has one thousand petals, hence the name, Thousand Petaled Lotus of the Crown Chakra. The Lotus can re-calibrate the energies of the Higher Realms. At times, it can host the presence of our soul and higher aspects of Self all the way to the Presence of the I Am That I Am and beyond.

When an essence from the Presence of the I Am That I Am is called to reside inside the lotus, we can receive the wealth of the wisdom of the universe, first hand, directed from inside the lotus on our crown to our body. This would be like sitting in the presence of your teacher and receiving continuous guidance and wisdom.

MEDITATIONAL JOURNEY
TO THE GOLDEN THRONE OF YHWH

Adonai my Beloveds, I am Jeshua Ben Joseph.

Visualize yourself standing in front of me. Focus your energy in the middle of your chest; at the center of your Heart Chakra. Imagine that White Light is pouring out of my Heart and entering your Heart. Visualize a Pillar of White Light forming around your body and mine. Visualize yourself merging into the essence of Jeshua Ben Joseph inside the Pillar of White Light. The Pillar extends above your head and continues to ascend, all the way to the Throne of the I Am That I Am in the thirteenth dimension of reality. We will begin to move upward inside the Pillar of Pure White Light to reach the Throne of the I Am That I Am.

We reach the Throne and you see Brilliant Light emanating from every direction as if a brilliant sun is shining upon you from the Throne. Feel the Perfected Presence of your own I Am That I Am, God in Form. Ask for your wishes to be granted. Ask for yourself, for humankind and for the future of Earth. Say,

"I ask for the release of negativity and lower vibrations from human beings and Earth. I especially ask for a clearing from the environments in which I work and from people, places and things which I communicate and come in contact with. I ask for the release of all darkness from the energy bodies of Earth and from the bodies of humankind. I ask for the alignment of the will of the world leaders with the Will of God. I ask for the Original Divine Blueprint of the Divine Will to be downloaded to Earth and anchored within the collective consciousness of humankind."

Pause while the Blueprint is being downloaded and visualize that a shower of Brilliant Light is pouring down to you. As you stand before the Throne of the I Am That I Am, you can begin to see the silhouette of the Presence of the I Am calling you to merge into the shower of Light with it. As you feel yourself immersed into the Presence. Say,

"Give me this through the intercession of Jeshua Ben Joseph. I especially ask for my own consciousness to be raised to levels where I can uphold the energies of Divine Will. I offer you my Will in total surrender. I ask that my Will be aligned with your Will. Not my Will but Thy Will be done. Your Will is now my Will. I relinquish my Free Will to you. What you Will for me is above and beyond the limitation of my personal Will. I choose your Will for me. Not my Will but Thy Will be done, aligning my Will with your Divine Will, I surrender my Will to you; you are all that I Am, I Am as you are, I Am That I Am; I Am, I Am, I Am."

Pause and breathe the Presence of the I Am into your lungs. Bring the energy of the Presence into your body. Feel yourself in Oneness with the Presence. Feel your small self dissolve into the Great Self of the I Am, as a drop returning to the ocean. Visualize that the power and might of the ocean is now behind you. Feel yourself in Oneness with the I Am. The microcosm who is you is now merged in Oneness with the macrocosm which is the Perfected Presence of the I Am That I Am. See yourself emerge out of that Oneness fully refreshed and revived. Visualize yourself embodying the Original Blueprint of the Divine Will from this moment on.

Now we will return inside the Pillar of Light. Before we take our leave from the Presence, invite the Presence to act through you. Remind yourself that you are a drop from the ocean of the I Am. Ask for the power, might, Will and the Life Force of the I Am to accompany you from this day on.

We bow down before the Presence at the Throne and take our leave with joy and gratitude. We return to stand inside of the Pillar of White Light. This time we will ascend to the twenty-second realm of reality to visit the Throne of YHWH.

See yourself ascending inside of the Pillar of Light. We become lighter as we move upward. The Light becomes more brilliant. Golden Shimmering Lights welcome us into this realm. We enter the energies of the Golden Throne. This is the Throne of Grace. The Presence of YHWH is seated at this Throne. The Twenty-Four Elders, also known as the Ancient of Days, are seated around in a circle. Four creatures are standing guard at the four directions, one with the face of a lion, another, a horse, the third an eagle and the fourth an ox. The Twenty-Four Elders sing the song of *"Holy, Holy, Holy is the Lord God of Hosts"*. With each chant of the Holy name, the Bright Light begins to pulse through the

Throne and from the Throne in every direction. Visualize yourself standing quietly and reverently waiting to be announced. I will go before you to announce your presence. You may stand and bathe in the Golden Shower of Light emanating from the Throne for a moment. Pause and take a deep breath.

You are now called to come forth and stand at the center before the Golden Throne of YHWH. A wave of blissful energy is emanating from the Throne to you. At first, all is Brilliant Golden Light. The Light is too brilliant for your eyes to recognize the form of YHWH seated at the Throne.

As you bathe in this Golden Shower of Bliss, you begin to notice an immensely Illuminated Being of Golden Light seated at the Throne. You move closer to stand a foot away from the Presence of YHWH. You stand in reverence and awe. The bliss and love from the Presence pulls you closer and you kneel down.

Now your head is on the Golden Liquid Light of YHWH's lap. You feel yourself showered with Light, your body embraced with love and your entire being immersed in the bliss of Brilliant Golden Light. You hear the sound of the chant from all around the Throne; *"Holy, Holy, Holy, is the Lord God of Hosts".* You are bathing in the Golden Light and immersed in the Bliss of the Presence of YHWH.

Now express your desires and ask for your personal and global intentions. Say,

"I offer myself to you and your Light. I ask for the Light of your Divine Will, Divine Wisdom and Divine Love to shine upon me from this day on. I offer my Will to you in total surrender and obedience. Not my Will but Thy Will be

done. Give me the Grace to receive your Light; to be your Light and to shine your Light on Earth. Give me the Grace to touch all souls with the brightness of your Light and with the shower of Grace from your Throne. Make me the messenger of your love, your Light, your Grace, your Wisdom and your Will on Earth. Over-light me with your own Presence and allow me to bring your Presence back down to Earth and to all souls. Give me the Grace to be the emissary of your Light on Earth. Align my Will with your Will. I surrender, I trust, I obey and I accept your Will as my Will. My will is Thy Will, Thy Will be done, so it is, it is done, Amen."

Stay and bathe in these energies. Ask for your specific and personal requests, or just be still in the bliss. Pause and take a deep breath.

We will now take our leave from the Presence of YHWH. Stand up and bow before the Presence as you step away. In reverence and gratitude, we bow down. Before we leave, I ask on your behalf that from this day on you will be allowed to come before the Throne of YHWH to receive blessings and to be showered with the Golden Light of Bliss. From this day on, I ask on your behalf for the Grace to live in surrender, trust, obedience and acceptance of the Light, love and wisdom of YHWH.

I ask and intercede on your behalf that you may remain connected to the Presence of YHWH and receive a direct shower of Golden Light from the Throne to keep you safe from harm and to hold you in the higher vibration of this Golden Light at all times.

We leave the Throne and return to the Pillar of White Light to descend down the dimensions and return to the consciousness of the body. We pause as we reach back to the thirteenth dimension at the Throne of the I Am That I Am. Ask once again for the Blessing and the Light, from the Presence of the I Am, to accompany you back to the consciousness of the body. Ask for the energy essence of the I Am to travel down the Pillar of Light to sit inside the lotus of your Crown Chakra at the top of your head. In this way, you will be connected directly to the Presence of the I Am That I Am. You will receive the higher energies from the Presence of the I Am That I Am through the lotus flower over your Crown Chakra. The wisdom and inner guidance is recalibrated by the lotus and sent to the chakras of your body. Guidance sent by the Presence of the I Am moves from the lotus of the Crown to the consciousness of the body.

The request is accepted. Therefore, in the company of the essence of the I Am, we travel down the Pillar of Light back to the consciousness of your body. As we move down to reach the Crown Chakra, a Bright Star begins to form above your head at your Crown Chakra. This star will carry the essence of I Am That I Am and sit directly at the center of the lotus flower which is the energetic abode of the lotus of your Crown Chakra. It will hold the essence of the I Am That I Am from this day on.

By repeating this exercise you can accelerate on the path of spiritual growth and Enlightenment. You will open up and cleanse your higher chakras to reach to the Thrones of the I Am That I Am and YHWH and build the bridge to your God-Self. These are steps to awaken you to higher levels of initiation on the path to Enlightenment. You have been working for eons of time to come to this point and to reach this day. I welcome you to this auspicious point on your journey.

Know that there are levels of more Brilliant White Light which exist beyond this realm, and you can visit those realms. Set out your intention to be taken to those realms in dreamtime. First you will recall events at subconscious levels and then bring those memories from the subconscious to the conscious level. To assist you, the Masters will work with you in dreamtime. When you are asleep, your consciousness is more receptive to the teachings than when you are awake, as the mind and emotions remain unattached and cause no interference. In dreamtime, with the help of the Masters, your consciousness can be expanded. In time, the memories of events can gradually seep into your wakeful consciousness. This will accelerate you on your journey to greater Light.

I hold you in my own heart with great love, joy and celebration. I congratulate you for all your efforts, and the joy, surrender and obedience with which you do this work. Remember, obedience and humility are two important factors in reaching Enlightenment.

With all of my heart I am your own Jeshua Ben Joseph. So it is.

CHAPTER III

Karma and Karmic Entanglement

This is an exercise in the form of a transformational candle grid given by Goddess Hecate. Its objective is to transform negativity, to release karmic entanglements, to accelerate us out of the dross and march us into the Light to bring forth our Divinely Ordained Mission as Earth's new cycle begins.

The moment when the sun goes into the equator is the true point of entering into a new year, the first day of spring or March Equinox (20-22 of March). It is an ancient tradition brought to Earth by Sanat Kumara, that we celebrate the birth of a new year and the rebirthing for all souls at March Equinox. The last time Sanat Kumara allowed a fragment of his own soul to take physical embodiment was as the being called Zoroaster, also known as Zarathustra. Zoroaster brought the knowledge and wisdom of performing ceremony and ritual in honor of Earth's birthday and to welcome the return of life and the victory of Light over Darkness. That was 8,000 years ago. His followers, known as Zoroastrians, have kept his teachings alive and continue to apply them to this day. The Spring Equinox and the re-birthing of Mother Earth prompt us to do some internal spring-cleaning. Letting go of old habits which no longer serve us and cleaning out the closets of the cobwebs — literally and metaphorically — will make way for, and bring in, greater Light.

Goddess Hecate blesses us with beautiful invocations to use in conjunction with this Candle Grid. These invocations will accelerate the release of karma and the downloading of the Original Blueprint as Divinely Ordained. When Light is everywhere, we can drop the dross, let go of karma and accelerate our return to our Original Divine Mission. With greater Light we can stop struggling to survive and can live to serve; performing our Divinely Ordained Mission.

CANDLE GRID TO RELEASE KARMA
AND KARMIC ENTANGLEMENTS

My Children of glory, I am Hecate.

I have come to give you a Transformational Candle Grid using the power of the Rays of Purple and Gold. This is a grid for acceleration. You need acceleration to move from karmic entanglements to your Divinely Ordained Mission; to be done with karma, pain and struggles.

For this grid, use three purple candles and three gold candles. The purple candle is for clearing of the Feminine Aspect and transmuting the emotional body dross, the energy of feelings and emotions. The gold is for clearing the Masculine Aspect and transmuting the mental body dross, the energy of actions and events relating to people, places and things. You will need yellow, purple and gold colored poster board. Cut a circle twelve inches in diameter out of the purple poster board and place it on a rectangular yellow poster board. Then cut an equilateral triangle out of the gold, approximately twelve inches on each side. Place this triangle inside of the purple circle. Place the three purple candles on three points around the circle and three gold candles on the three points of the triangle. In this way every other candle is gold and purple. You use tall, large candles; or small votives and replace them as they run out. You are setting the same intentions every day for twenty-two consecutive days or for the entire month.

Charging Your Candle Grid

Begin with the first purple candle and move clockwise around the grid formation. Hold the first purple candle up and read the invocation given below. Moving clockwise, go to the next candle which is gold, and repeat the same invocation. Go around the grid clockwise and repeat the invocation for each candle until you return to where you started. In the invocation we shall seek help from the Thrones. We first go to the Throne of the I Am That I Am, God in Form, then to the Throne of YHWH and finally to the Throne of Undifferentiated Source, God in Non-form. Take a deep breath.

Say out loud and in a commanding voice,

"I ask for the transmutation and release of all karmic entanglements with people, places and things. In the name of the I Am That I Am, God in Form, in the name of YHWH and the Throne of Grace and in the name of the Undifferentiated Source, God in Non-form, I ask for the installation of my Divinely Ordained Mission NOW. I ask this to become my ultimate reality. I ask for people, places and things

who serve my Divine Mission to be brought into my life. Those that no longer serve my highest interest are to be released from my life. Their energy is to be cleared from my body, my emotions, my mind, my soul, my spirit, my life, my energy field and my environment NOW! I ask the intercession of the Masters, both living and ascended, and all aspects of the Divine Mother and her Creative Force. I call upon Goddesses Hecate, Pele, Quan Yin, Isis, Athena, Victory, Liberty and Mother Mary. I call upon the Archangels and all the Angelic Forces of Light together with Metatron and Melchizedek. I command the forces of the Five Elements to abide the Will of Divine Mother and to intercede on my behalf for this intention. I ask for my Divinely Ordained Mission to be downloaded to my body, being and life immediately (if you have a personal intention for the release of a karmic issue or situation related to people, relationships, career, finances, etc. state it here). I call forth the Template for the Original Blueprint for the Divinely Ordained Mission which will best serve and suit me to be downloaded into my life and my being, NOW. So it is."

Print or write this invocation and place it near your candle grid. Every time you light the candles, read the invocation and call to these beings to intercede on your behalf. Sit still by the grid and meditate on your intentions, asking the Divine Mother's Light and blessings to shower upon you.

When the candles are lit, the grid will continue to spread your intentions into the Environment, accelerating the outcome. If you are unable to light the candle grid every day, or do not have the time to sit with your grid, use this powerful invocation and the statement of your intentions to work on your behalf. Carry the invocation around with you and say it as many times as you can each day. It is more important to say the intention on a daily basis than to light the candles. Keep your intentions in your own heart and mind and say them with or without lighting the candle grid.

Do this grid for twenty-two consecutive days to anchor the energy. If after twenty-two days you feel complete, then you have anchored the energies. You may continue for a longer period of time until you feel that you have fully anchored the energies or you feel you have received the answers to your desires. The longer you continue this grid, the more powerful it will become.

My Children, I bless you with all of my heart,
I am your Mother, Hecate, Blessed be.

Candle Grid to Release Karma and Karmic Entanglements

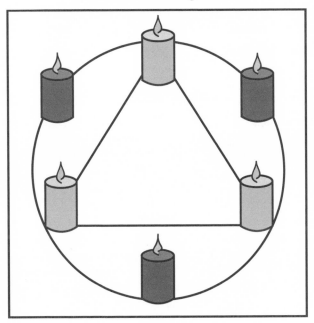

Summary of Candle Grid

Materials Needed

- Yellow poster board
- Purple circle (12" in diameter) cut out of paper or poster board
- Gold triangle (12" on each side) cut out of paper or poster board
- 3 gold candles
- 3 purple candles

Instructions for Creating the Candle Grid

1. On yellow poster board, place the purple-colored circle made out of paper/poster board.
2. Inside the circle place a triangle in gold-colored paper/poster board.
3. Place the 3 purple candles on three points of the outside circle.
4. Place the 3 gold candles on the three points of the inside triangle.
5. Beginning with a purple candle, hold the candle up and state your intentions.
6. Moving clockwise, hold up the next gold candle and repeat the intentions. Continue clockwise with each candle until you return to the starting point.
7. Now light each candle in the same order that you imbued them.
8. Repeat the invocation as presented above.
9. Do this grid for twenty two days.

CHAPTER IV

RELEASING NEGATIVITY

St. Germain is the Master or Cohan of the Seventh Ray, the Violet Flame of Transmutation. In this chapter, for the month of April, he gives a beautiful discourse on keeping our thoughts and actions clear from negativity. He offers us prayers and invocations before the Thrones of God and through the intercession of the Masters of Light.

Also in the month of April, please remember that our own beloved Metatron has appointed the twenty-fourth of April of each year as the Ascension Day (See Book I, Chapter IV of *Path to Enlightenment; The Pillar of Light*, for more details on Ascension Day). Remember to invoke his presence and the presence of all the Masters of Light and Wisdom around this time and ask for the removal of all karmic entanglements and transmutation of all dross which stands in the way of our Enlightenment. Know that we can move our consciousness to a higher vibration and ascend above the pain and struggles of this Earthly realm. This does not mean that we will have to die or leave the Earth plane but that we will ascend duality and leave separation to reach God-Unity and Enlightenment, while still residing on Earth in our physical bodies.

HOLDING NEGATIVE AND POSITIVE ENERGIES

Beloveds, I am St. Germain.

The only way to reach Enlightenment is to release all darkness. This feat can be attained by relinquishing power from darkness and returning to Light. Let that be your Guiding Light. You may be holding onto a negative energy such as jealousy, greed, laziness or fear. It will stand in your way of gaining greater Light. You may be able to hide your jealousy for a day or a lifetime. You may even be able to hide it for ten lifetimes. The truth is, wherever it is hidden, it is spreading darkness. Where there is darkness, there is no Light. If there is no Light to take you to the higher levels, you will stay and become stagnant.

If you never thought of the importance of releasing negative energies from your own being, now is a good time to adopt this new way of thinking. Yes, you can make do by keeping some of your fears, some of your envy, some of your jealousy, some of your greed and some of your laziness. You might even reach high positions in the mundane world, but you will never gain full Enlightenment until all of those qualities have been fully released and the Life Force which moves you and guides you has fully adopted the Light. The Life Force, by its essence, is Pure White Light. Because of the density of the third dimensional reality of present day Earth, all life forms are spinning slower and have adopted levels of darkness. This leads people to believe they may be able to get away with their negativity. That is a false impression. Until you are almost one hundred percent Light, you will not gain true Enlightenment. It is true that while you are in physical embodiment you cannot gain one hundred percent Light because a body of matter inherently has some darkness. It holds darkness as it solidifies to become form. That can account for a small percentage of darkness. Yet your ultimate goal should be to attain Pure White Light and leave all negativity and darkness.

One negative word, one negative thought, one negative impression or expression, leaves its mark in your energy field and lowers your Quotient or percentage of Light. It makes no difference to us how you live your day and whether you stay positive or not. It makes a great difference to you, the energy field which emanates around you and those energy fields you attract to yourself. When you stay positive and take into account the importance of holding the Light and not giving in to the darkness of negativity, you allow a greater transmission of Light in your immediate environment. When you keep your thoughts pure and clean, you are stopping negativity from permeating inside as well as around you.

You may think, what is the use of distracting myself from this darkness when I truly feel the darkness of pain, struggle or despair? The answer is, the more you focus on the darkness, the more darkness you will pull into your energy field. Negative, angry, sad, depressed thoughts magnify the negativity and add to the darkness that is pulled to your energy field. A moment of weakness may bring you a dark thought. By distracting yourself from that thought and not expressing it in words or actions, you allow the environment to stay focused on The Light and you keep the Light permeating around you. That Light can then help to release the darkness from within and around you. Think of this at all times. Persevere in your thoughts, in your words, and in your actions to remain focused on The Light. Persevere on uprooting the dark emotions from inside your being; persevere in harnessing all feelings and emotions from being spewed out in uncontrollable words or actions. Remind yourself that one moment of control can bring great benefits.

Slipping into fear, which is a negative emotion, can create an avalanche of dark energy around you. The length of time and the amount of energy that will then be required to release and to clear that darkness from around you could be spent in uplifting you and assisting you to serve The Light. To do this, say the following,

"I ask with all of my might, with the full force of my intention, with all of my love and with all of my mind's power that I be assisted in releasing all darkness from within me. I release darkness from my words, from my actions, from my thoughts and from my energy bodies. I ask that my focus be constantly pulled to The Light. I ask that Guardians of Light be appointed to protect me from slipping into darkness. In the name of the I Am That I Am, in the name of Light, through the intercession of St. Germain, I ask Guardians of Light and Masters of Light and Wisdom to be appointed to protect me from slipping into darkness of emotional negativity, mental negativity, spiritual negativity, physical negativity and negative actions."

Every sickness in your body is a physical negativity. It becomes a sickness when the mental, emotional and physical negativity attacks your healthy body. From cancer to a simple flu or a cold, all are the outcome of allowing negativity into the body. Do not blame yourself for moments of weakness. That would be adding more fuel to the fire of negativity. Simply stay positive, love yourself in the moments of weakness more than in your moments of glory because it is in the moments of weakness that you need love. Who can give you greater love than yourself? Your own self is the Self of All. There is no satisfaction greater than receiving love from your own self. When you find you have slipped, love yourself and encourage yourself to come back to the Light. Do not beat yourself up; do not give in to further fears and negativities. Pull Light to your energy field and spread it to all. Do not take no for an answer, whether you are standing before the Presence of the Throne of God or before a mere child who is resisting transmission of Light. If you feel that God is depriving you of Light, then demand it, ask, supplicate, request, and beg if you have to. Do whatever it takes to re-stabilize yourself in Greater Light. If a child is resisting to give to you or to receive from you, give it love. In love the resistance dissolves. Treat yourself like a needy child, deserving of your love. That same love you can take to your brothers and sisters of the Ascended Realms, the Masters. That does not mean you give up your power. On the contrary, love is a powerful weapon. It can annihilate all darkness, it can remove all barriers. With love, all things are possible. Turn that love inside to yourself, especially when you are displeased with yourself. Do not allow a moment of displeasure to lead you to greater darkness.

MEDITATION TO RELEASE DARKNESS
FROM BODY, MIND, EMOTIONS AND SOUL

I now invite you to come with me to the Throne of the I Am That I Am. We stand before the Throne and say,

"We ask for the annihilation of all acts, words and thoughts of evil; relinquishment of the power of the Dark Lords and their dominion over all physical, emotional, mental and spiritual bodies of all species and all souls. We ask for the re-establishment of the reign of the Lords of Light. We ask that the Guardianship of Earth, all beings and all things be given to the Lords of Light. We ask this from the Throne of the I Am That I Am. Furthermore, we ask for the Quotient of Light for all species of the Earth plane and the planet herself to increase. This will then raise the consciousness and the Quotient of Light for the substance and the physical matter of all souls, all places and all things. We ask for the integration of Light into the mind, the soul and the spirit of all things manifest and un-manifest." Now pause and ask for your own personal intentions and desires. Take a deep breath.

Pause and allow the release to begin. Say,

"I intend that the healing release will now begin for my being and for all souls and the planetary body and matter of Earth."

Next we move through the Throne of YHWH and bathe in the Light of the Presence of YHWH. We ask the Presence to accompany us to the Throne of Undifferentiated Source and to help bring our petition to this Throne. The Throne of Undifferentiated Source is the non-manifest Presence of God-Source. In this level all is Pure White Light. We stand before this Presence and offer all that we have and all that we are. Say,

"We ask for the annihilation of all negativity and all evil and we ask for the relinquishment of the power from the lower vibrational forces and the restoration of power of the Lords of Light as Guardians of Earth and all souls, of this entire Solar System and beyond.

We ask for the highest Quotient of Light which the Earth can absorb in each given moment to be released to Earth from this moment on. We ask this through the intercession of all the Light Beings in the Presence of the I Am That I Am, YHWH and from the Throne of the Undifferentiated Source.

We ask for the Presence of the Seven Mighty Elohim, the architects of this entire Solar System, to intercede on our behalf.

We ask for the Presence of the Great Silent Watchers, the God-Mother for this Earth and all souls, who held the thought-form for the creation of this planet, to intercede on our behalf.

We ask on behalf of all manifest and non-manifest Creation that the reign of Light may fully establish its presence on Earth and throughout the Solar System, this Galaxy, the Milky Way, the universe, the conglomerate of universes and into the cosmos.

We ask the Throne of the Undifferentiated Source to extend the dispensation for Light to raise its quotient; weaving a fabric of Greater Light throughout the manifest and non-manifest conglomerates of planets, star systems, galaxies and cosmos.

We ask this in the name of Light, in the name of all Life Force, whose sustenance depends on Light. We ask this in service to The Light.

We ask for the blessing and the approval from the Throne of the Undifferentiated Source."

Pause now and take a deep breath. (State your own personal intentions and desires again here).

We receive the Grace and the Blessing from the Throne of the Undifferentiated Source. We take our leave now. I guide you to begin to spiral down from the Presence of the Undifferentiated Source back through the Throne of YHWH, to the Presence of the I Am That I Am, and into our bodies. Take a deep breath.

I hold you all in my heart. A great shift in your Quotient of Light will begin to happen with the practice of this exercise. Repeat this exercise for twenty-two days for completion. I will be with you every step of the way. Call upon me to walk with you and say these invocations with me. Remember that as the Cohan of the Seventh Ray, the Violet Ray of Transmutation, I can intercede on your behalf. As the Maha Cohan for the next 98,000 Year Cycle of Light, I will be able to work with you through the time and space continuum for all the events that will transpire in the future for humanity and the planet. It is my honor to offer you this opportunity. I do hope that you realize the importance of this gift of acceleration into Greater Light.

With great love and in the joy of this togetherness, I hold you in my own heart.

I am St. Germain. So it is.

CHAPTER V

TRUTH AND NEGATIVITY

In this discourse, Metatron provides us with insight into the energies that Earth and humanity are experiencing at this juncture of our evolution. Many people are perplexed by the upheavals and unusual events they are seeing around them and in their own lives. There is chaos and suffering from the natural disasters hitting the planet across the globe impacting the lives of all of us. Those who are awakened are seeking guidance from the Masters. Those who have not been awakened are now stirring out of their unconscious sleep and waking up to higher spiritual Truths. It is, therefore, appropriate to understand the present events and prepare for the times ahead, as well as the peace that will follow, according to Metatron.

The month of May is like opening the door to summer; the seeds planted in spring are beginning to take root and bear fruit. We are planting seeds of Light. To help them germinate and grow, we must pull out the weeds of negativity and dross. When brought to the surface, we are able to release our dross. This opportunity for release is a blessing as we collectively let go of layers of heaviness to allow more of our true essence and Light to shine, blessing Mother Earth and all of humanity. The entire month of May is offered to our beloved Mother Mary. Therefore, remember to call upon her to intercede on your behalf in all your endeavors.

The full moon of May is a time to celebrate Wesak, also known as Lord Buddha's day. A powerful vortex of energy opens at this time as Lord Buddha, Mother Mary and other Ascended Masters gather close to Earth to bestow their blessings upon us all. May their Light and blessings carry you to brighter Light.

The Impact of Solar Energies in Replacing Negativity with Truth

Beloveds of my own heart, I am Metatron.

Since September of 2001, the Earth energies have been shifting in a new direction and in a different way. The September 11th event was believed by some to be a global event of enormous proportion, and I tend to agree. With it, a new cycle of behavior opened up and a new test for the consciousness of humankind. You reached a point where everyone felt the thread that binds humanity together. A favorite statement of mine is, *"All is One and One is All"*. The pain and struggles of one faction of society is the pain and struggle of all. No one can inflict pain and struggle upon another without suffering themselves. That was the lesson of the events of September 11th. The world has not come to know peace yet, and the collective consciousness of humankind must realize that every human being, every country and every continent are organs of the same body and parts of the same whole. In that sense, what effects one part affects all parts. Until that realization becomes a Universal Truth, understood by the masses, the struggle will continue.

To succeed in awakening humanity to the understanding of the Truth, the Divine Ray of Truth will need to be anchored. This will result in illuminating the Divine Spark, which is the Light of Truth, within the hearts of all humankind. For as long as we have not reached the point where Truth is upheld, the collective consciousness of humankind will not awaken and critical mass will not be reached. Upon full awakening, one percent of the population of Earth will illuminate that Divine spark within their hearts. Then critical mass is reached. The landmark date of entering that point was set for March Equinox of 2005. At that point, the seed was planted. By March Equinox of 2006, we were on our way to critical mass. Completion of that event took until March Equinox of 2007. Important events of planetary caliber transpire during the Month of March. This is why the weeks leading up to, during and after March can be difficult and trying times.

For Earth to cleanse herself of her dross and begin to live up to her true and pure Original Intent, it must first allow the energies of betrayal, abandonment, rejection, and anger to come to the surface. The release begins from March and continues to Summer Solstice which is the zenith point for these energies to come to the surface. Summer Solstice will have the fire of anger brewing as that is the energy the Earth and the collective consciousness of humankind need to release. There are Solar energies beaming their Light and power to the Earth for this exact reason. Full moons and new moons are times of intense bombardment of solar energies which release negativity from the collective consciousness of humankind and from the crust of the Earth.

From the time of the Summer Solstice, around June 19-22, until Fall Equinox, September 19-22, we will move to anchor the energies of Truth. We must empty the cup of the poison before we can fill it with nectar. Anger and fear are poisonous substances, which must be released from the cup which is your body.

From mid-August into September and October there will be peace. You will all feel your contracted muscles relax and you can sleep at night. This is the point of filling the cup with the nectar. Your bodies will absorb and anchor peace. When the anchoring of the energies of peace is complete, we will go into yet another cycle, which begins around November. November is always a time for a new cycle to begin. Whatever has preceded it would set the pace for what is yet to come. Fortunately, the struggles with all the negativities will be over and a point of stillness can be reached. By the time the feast of Thanksgiving arrives, on the third week of November, many souls will be ready to step up to higher spiritual paths because of the enormous growth gained through the year. There are many initiation ceremonies conducted presently by the Masters who take their students to the fifth and higher dimensional realms to receive initiations and teachings. The Masters are involved in raising the collective consciousness of humankind during dreamtime. This is especially the case with souls who are moving through higher levels of initiation and are being prepared to reach Enlightenment while in the physical body. Then, you would experience peace. This means that the cycle begins with upheaval and ends with peace and harmony if all goes well. This is the case with every new seven year cycle. 2008 denotes entry into a new cycle of Seven years. That cycle ends to begin the next one on 2015 and so forth.

The year 2012 is believed to be a point where time as you know it would be coming to an end. This belief could be considered accurate if it is understood correctly. Time as you know it can come to an end. This linear time is the product of polluted densities, which cause you grief and turmoil and pain. It has a hold on you. The analogy of it is the story of the frog. If you put a frog in hot boiling water it will jump out and run away; it will not stand for the pain and refuse to struggle in the hot water. However, if the frog was placed in lukewarm water and then gradually and gently the water started heating up, the frog would acclimate to the conditions. Then, even at the boiling point, the frog will not jump out of the water because it would be conditioned to that environment and all would seem natural to the frog.

The water, which represents the Earth's conditions, is boiling all around you and none of you are jumping out. Even if some of you did, where would you go? This has been a gradual process; even though it is practically unbearable, you have accepted it as natural up until now. You are still sitting around waiting for the other shoe to drop, waiting to see what will happen next. With the guidance from the Masters, it is our hope that the collective consciousness of humankind will reach a point where you realize your situation and begin to find a way to stop the harsh conditions. You do not have the choice to jump out of the world and go elsewhere, yet you do have the choice to stop the pain. By going back to the source and the root cause of the pain, you can fix the conditions which you have accepted and taken for granted for so long. By running away you will not achieve as much as you would by staying put and fixing the problem.

To fix the problem you must first face the fact that there are conditions which are no longer acceptable. Pain, struggle, fear, deception, untruths and such must stop running your world and affecting your life. To fix the problems your collective will must align to choose joy, peace and harmony. The Ascended Masters of Light and the Masters of Wisdom are offering their service to guide you out of this dross in all ways. Their help will accelerate your growth to collectively choose to divert the pain and turn your attention to reinstating peace and joy. Living in alignment with the Divine Will, you can remember yourself as the Divine Self, One with the Source. Allowing and willing yourself to be empowered, calling love, Light and peace from the Source is the key. Your Guides, Angelic Forces, Ascended Masters and physically embodied Masters of Light and Wisdom are offering you their service to accelerate you on the path of growth and Enlightenment.

Take every opportunity to place yourself in the physical presence of the living Masters and call upon the Ascended Masters and your Guardian Angels for guidance and wisdom. Read all you can on spiritually illuminating articles and books, and use them as source-guides to direct you. Find out which among them has a closer connection with you. Your Master Guides, your Angelic Hosts, your Guardian Angels, your Ray and the Cohan of your Ray and work with them. Simply ask, pray and invoke your Primary Master Guides and the Cohan of your Ray. It is absolutely true that *"When the student is ready the teacher will reveal herself/himself."* All you need to do is ask with a sincere heart and an open mind. You will be led. Ask that you are given the Grace to choose joy, peace and harmony. Ask that you let go of pain and misery. Ask that the teachers reveal themselves and ask that you be receptive to them. Ask through the intercession of Metatron. I am at your service. I will help and guide you.

I am your very own Metatron. So it is.

"I call forth the Flame of God-Unity
to be established in my Cosmic Heart."
Archangel Michael

CHAPTER VI

FORGIVENESS

This is an invocational mantra given by Metatron to release karmic entanglements. Metatron explains that we can free ourselves from the pain and dross of these entanglements by going into Oneness and by loving and honoring all we encounter.

June is the beginning of summer in the Northern Hemisphere and winter in the Southern Hemisphere and a time to celebrate Solstice. The entry and exit point to the Light. By releasing ourselves of all our dross, we allow our Light to shine, sharing our true essence and love with Mother Earth.

With such a rich celebration of life, it is an excellent time to heed the words of Metatron, repeating this mantra with an open, loving heart as you feel the pain and dross melt away into Oneness. Light, love and blessings of the Masters will accompany us along the way.

With great love I wish you a wonderful Solstice celebration and a season of joy.

Prayer for Forgiveness

Beloveds of my own heart, I am Metatron, El-Shaddai. Take a deep breath with me.

Focus your energy in your Solar Plexus. I will begin to administer healing upon you to clear your body of painful and harmful emotions, thoughts and physical symptoms which are caused by karmic entanglements. I will help to release the root cause of such entanglements from your body.

The Laws of the universe are based on justice and fairness; the laws of your planet too are based on just reaction for every action. Two or more people may come together to resolve their karmic entanglements. They remain involved with each other until their karma is complete. However, when one of them has learned his/her lessons, then he/she can be released from the karmic situation, even when the other party or parties are not free from the karma or the issue. Know this fact, learn to free yourself from the karma and allow yourself to move on to bigger and better things.

Life on planet Earth is based on Free Will. This means that human beings have a right to will themselves in or out of any situation at any time. Even though you may feel stuck in some situations, with your Free Will you can move on at any time. However, it is best to move on when you have released your karmic entanglements and have closure. Because when you quit, when you can no longer take it anymore and decide to move on, you will be taking the entire karmic situation with you and deferring it to another round in this lifetime or other lifetimes. It is best, therefore, to deal with karmic issues at the first go-around, in this lifetime if possible and not postpone it to another lifetime. It takes less effort and energy to complete something once and for all, than to come back and do everything all over again. It is also better to learn the lessons the first time around and not differ to second and third rounds.

You can use the following exercise to free yourself from the pain and heartache from various situations. You may have already moved on from the relationship but the heartache may still linger. Forgiveness is the healing balm to help you have complete closure. It will also help to ease already existing situations. If you are in relationships with people where your interactions are not harmonious or easy and smooth, you can repeat this invocational prayer. By releasing the karmic debts from the situation, the burdens are removed and ease and peace is installed. A difficult situation will then become pleasant and harmonious, the encounters will become peaceful and harmonious and the outcome loving and nurturing.

To begin, you must first go to the root cause of the karmic entanglement and release it. Start by stating that whatever brought up the conflict or disharmony, consider it paid off now. No more payback is necessary. No more arguments, unpleasant encounters or further dialogue is necessary. Be prepared to accept that not even apologies are necessary. In some cases where you may want to have complete closure with no further contact, you may state that no more encounters are necessary in regards to this specific situation.

Sometimes people become angry at each other and say, *"I do not want to see you ever again, not even in any other lifetime; not even if you come back to serve me and pay what you owe me."* While it is possible to see the merit in this while you are in physical embodiment, it poses limitations. You may be depriving yourself of an opportunity to be served and another person the opportunity of offering you service in order to make up for their previous shortcomings and karmic debt.

The best course of action where there is karmic entanglement is to face the situation, embrace the possibility of resolving it through compassion and forgiveness and to release the situation through prayer, intention and will. Remember that any situation can be dealt with from its web of karmic and human ego-based perspective. On the other hand, it can be handled from the Divinely Ordained and compassionate perspective. Some situations or relationships are strictly karmic, and when the karma is released, the people are free from each other or from the situation. In others, the situation or the relationship may continue, once the karma is released in a harmonious and amicable way. Our aim is to end the strictly karmic situations which serve no good purpose and stop them from bringing about greater harm (*e.g.,* a difficult career which is going nowhere, a relationship which has gone sour where every encounter brings about more conflict leading to more karmic entanglements). Our aim is also to bring harmony to, and the continuation of, beneficial relationships or situations (e.g., a parent-child relationship which has gone sour). For this purpose, I have brought you the following prayer for release of karmic entanglements and freedom from pain and struggle.

Prayer for Forgiveness and Release from Karmic Entanglements

I forgive myself,
I forgive you,
And I ask for a complete healing for both/all of us.
At all levels of our being-ness,
In all our Five Body Systems,
I ask for our healing.
Never again will I be affected, distracted, delayed by your actions,
by our interactions and you by mine.
I hold you in the Light
I hold you in Divine Love
I hold you in Divine Power
I hold you in Divine Wisdom
I call forth the Threefold Flame of Love, Wisdom and Power,
I release you into it.
Whatever lessons you and I have agreed to learn from one another in this lifetime,
I ask that I learn them in joy,
I pray that you shall learn them in joy.
I offer Light from the core of my heart,
Pure White Light to heal you and to heal me.
I call forth the Pure White Light from the Presence of the I Am That I Am
To descend upon my heart and your heart,

I forgive you for all the moments that I have felt betrayed by you.
I forgive you for all the moments that I have felt hurt by you.
I forgive you for all the moments that my emotions have brought out the worst in me
Because of what you have done.
I forgive you for all the moments that my thoughts have been
of lower vibration directed at you.
I forgive myself
For all the lower thoughts I have sent to you.
For all the lower emotions I have directed at you.
For all the physical pain I have wished upon you.
For all the derogatory thoughts and actions that I have sent you
In my mind, in my heart, through my body and my being, I forgive myself.
I ask your forgiveness
For all I have done, all I have been and all I have caused.
On both our behalf, I ask in the name of the I Am That I Am, in the name of
YHWH, in the name of Undifferentiated Source,
Through the intercession of Christ Maitreya, our World Teacher,
In the name of Sanat Kumara, our Planetary Logos,
That we both may be forgiven
For all the friction, all the pain, all the trauma, all the distraction,
all the delay, all the separation
That we have caused upon each other and created as a reality
on Earth and outside of Earth
In all dimensions and realities.
I thank you with all of my heart for choosing to teach me the hardest lessons,
The lessons which I would otherwise not have faced nor learned.
I honor you for agreeing to play such an important role in my life.
Thank you for all your acts

Whatever their cause and however they may have played out
You have loved me with all of your heart, all of your soul;
why else would you agree to such a harsh lesson.
You have agreed to play such a difficult role, I respect every moment of time
and energy that you have bestowed upon our interaction
Which became a karmic entanglement
I now offer this karmic entanglement before God,
Before our Mother-Father-Child Self,
Before the Presence of the I Am That I Am, our own God Self in Form,
Before YHWH, the Golden Light of our soul,
Before Undifferentiated Source, the non-manifest Universal Consciousness.
I ask for a complete purification.
I ask for a clearing, cleansing and release of all
That has transpired between us, past, present, and future.
Whatever may transpire from this moment on,
I offer through the Three-Fold Flame of Divine Love,
Divine Wisdom and Divine Power to God.
For in God we are One, and to God in Oneness we shall return.
I ask that I may see God in you and see you as myself.
I ask that I may see myself worthy of God,
Worthy of being One with God,
Worthy of embodying God,
Worthy of knowing God,
Worthy of accepting God,
Worthy of becoming God,
Worthy of living in Oneness with God,
Side by side with you.
For you are a reflection of myself.

You are an externalization of my being.
What is within you is within me.
What goes on around you, goes on around me.
As we merge and unite in Oneness, our separation is ceased.
Our Oneness will bring all our differences to a close.
No darkness can ever penetrate between us.
There is no differentiation where I end and you begin.
I hold you in my own heart.
Your heart beats with the rhythm of the same God that I Am.
I Am That I Am within me is the emanation of the I Am That I Am within you.
In that I Am, I hold you.
I offer this togetherness to the Oneness.
Whatever is the Divine Will for you and for myself, I now call forth.
I invoke, I intend, I decree
That I accept myself as worthy of holding
The Oneness of God within you, God within me and God I Am,
Together, without separation from this moment on.
I ask this in the name of the I Am That I Am which I Am and you are.
So it is. It is done. Amen.

Apply the Truth of the above invocation. Apply the intention of it. Apply it by believing it from your heart and feeling its Truth through these words. Go into that Oneness and realize that the only way you can be free from any situation is to embrace it, embody it and become it. When you change your mindset, you shift from within. Then you change the microcosm. The microcosm reflects what is within it to the world around it, the macrocosm. Then the world around you has no other choice but to change. If it does not, then it is removed from being the world around you and it can no longer be a reality which you experience. That is when things change and you can walk away from bad situations.

Ultimately, the moment will come when you no longer feel the stickiness remain of any karmic entanglements. At that point, you have closure. Then you are free to leave. The Universe will provide you with the "out". It will point out the exit signs to you. Once that happens, not for one iota of a second will you have to stay longer. Neither as a sacrifice nor as an act of choice will you need to stay longer. Nor will you be inclined to stay around for greater lessons simply because greater lessons are waiting elsewhere. Until then, say these prayers and take the burden off of your shoulders and ask God to help you carry your burdens, or better still, ask God to transmute all your burdens and help you see the Oneness.

When you look in a mirror you see your own reflection. You cannot look in the mirror and see the reflection of someone else. Therefore, if within your own heart there is forgiveness; if within your own mind there is wholeness; if within yourself you can hold the image of perfection, then whatever is reflected in the mirror is perfection. For as long as you can see the perfection inside and out, you will be happy.

Sometimes two partners who love each other talk about each other's beauty. It may make others wonder how they see beauty in each other when, in the eyes of those who see the beauty as skin deep, there is no apparent beauty in the two partners. Yet the partners remain oblivious to the lack of beauty and to the imperfections in each other. They see the imperfections as perfect.

By the same token, you may have experienced an instance when you cannot trust a person or you feel uneasy in their presence, yet everyone else is saying, *"Oh, he/she is so beautiful, so beautiful; they are not only beautiful on the outside, they are beautiful on the inside."* You sit there and think, *"Oh, I can see the skin deep beauty, but it is leaving me unaffected. In fact, it is leaving me uneasy, and truth be known, I cannot even trust the beauty. I would rather know someone not so beautiful but one I can trust."* The macrocosm manifests realities which are the reflection of the microcosm. You are seeing your own fears, shortcomings or lack reflected in them. If you felt good about yourself, then it would not matter what or how that person looked or felt, even if indeed, they were not trustworthy. You would be able to accept their imperfections as perfect and not be threatened by it.

These Truths are important and integral parts of phases of your own spiritual growth. You can carry the burden for God diligently and refuse to put it down until you get home to God. Then, when you get home, you may be so tired that you forget that you have reached home. Or you can be so in love with God that you can forget the burden and let it go as you strive to get home and not even know that you left the burden behind. The truth is you have not left home. The old adage *"Home is where the heart is"* is so appropriate. Sometimes in our love for God, in our desire to serve, in our zest to make the most out of each lifetime, we end up over-doing, over-stretching and over-reacting. Then we think we do all of this to overcome the pain of separation.

Well, who said we are separate to begin with? What is separation? You are all fragments and aspects of God's own being. How can God be separate from the particles of its own being? If we can intellectually understand that everything is God, then how can anything be separate from God? If you can emotionally experience that everything is God, then you will know that there is no separation. This experience comes about not through the kind of knowledge you read in a book, but through wisdom you experience within your own heart.

I hold you in my own heart. Call upon me to show you the Oneness intellectually, but most importantly, mentally and emotionally. Call upon me to open your heart to the realization that we are all One and the Oneness stretches out from you, the fragment, to God, the Source of All. It will be my pleasure to watch your growth, it is a pleasure to walk by your side, and it will be a pleasure to bring you home to Oneness and free you from the pain of separation. In every moment as we continue together on the path of realizing the Oneness and as we get closer to living it, I hold you in my heart.

I am Metatron, El-Shaddai. So it is.

"For in God we are One,
and to God in Oneness we shall return."
Metatron

CHAPTER VII

REJUVENATION

This meditation is given by Metatron to help clear our physical bodies as we merge the Earth's Life Force energy with the Pure White Light of Source. Meditating outside and connecting with nature, while visualizing the Red Life Force as Metatron describes below, can be very powerful. We feel regenerated when we spend time out in the open with the Earth energies. Fertile ground is the perfect setting to work with this beautiful meditation and to merge the energies of Earthly realms with the energies of the Divine Realms. As the body is engulfed in the energies of Earth and Pure White Light, a wonderful physical healing takes place. Let this healing fill you with love and compassion for all living things. I wish you a wonderful month full of joy.

MEDITATION TO CLEANSE THE PHYSICAL BODY; MERGING THE RED LIFE FORCE WITH THE PURE WHITE LIGHT

Beloveds of my own heart, I am Metatron. Take a deep breath with me.

I would like you to open your heart to my love, and I will begin to clear your physical body of pain, pollution and dross. I will start the clearing from your left foot. You will feel the Red Earth Energy pulled up from the Heart-core of Mother Earth. It moves up to your left foot; from your left foot to your ankle, calf, knee, thigh to your left hip. The Red Life Force Energy moves up your torso on the left side of your body. You will feel it in your left shoulder, arm, hand and your fingers. Feel it fully on the entire left side of your body as it comes up.

I now call forth the Cylinder of Light which carries the Pure White Light of the Presence of the Undifferentiated Source to the I Am That I Am, down to you. That Pure Light will first reach to your Crown Chakra on top of your head. Then it enters your head cavity, filling your Third Eye. Filling your entire head with Pure Light, it reaches your throat. From the Throat Chakra, the Pure Light is mixed with the Red Life Force which is coming through the left side of your body. The Pure Light of the I Am and the Red Life Force Energy of Earth mix and create the Pink Light of Divine Love. Heaven and Earth come together through your body. This Pink Light Force then arches down to the right side of your body. It begins filling your right shoulder and your chest cavity. Even though this Pink Light Force is moving down the right side of your body, it fills your entire chest cavity. It fills and bathes all your organs in the Heavenly and Earthly Love Force and Life Force.

The Red Life Force of Mother Earth is like the blood which runs through your body. The color of your blood, the Life Force within your body when exposed to the element of air, is red. The Red Life Force Energy in your own body is now enhanced with the Life Force Energy of Earth. Visualize Pure White Light pouring down from your Crown Chakra and Red Life Force Energy coming up from the Earth. The Heavenly-Earthly Energies mix to become the Pink Light of Divine Love. The loving, nurturing Force of Light, becomes the Life Force which unites Heaven and Earth inside your body. This Pink Life Force will induce healing in all your organs.

The Pink Light of Divine Love will permeate every organ, every cell, every atom and every iota of your being. Through this meditation, the Divine and the mundane unite to fill you with love and to release duality.

This Pink Light permeates the entire Universe. It is the glue that binds all things together and brings the Creation into manifest physicality. This Love is the Life Force for the Spirit of all things. In the organ of the Heart, love abounds. In the Chakra of the Heart, the doors of the Palace of the Heart open up. In the Great Hall of the Palace, this Rose Pink Light permeates Divine Love in the center of your chest. It unites the Five Body System: the physical body, the etheric body, the emotional body, the mental body and the spiritual body. The past and the future are brought together to a point of manifestation in the present moment. Take a deep breath.

Focus on the organ of your Heart and your Heart Chakra, filling them with the Pink Light of Divine Love. Sit for a moment visualizing this magnificent picture. I call forth the Presence of the Divine Mother, she has many aspects. You can receive her in whatever form she chooses to show you. You can receive her in her form as Mother Mary, Goddess Hecate, Quan Yin, Pele, Isis, Athena or any other feminine form.

DIVINE MOTHER

Let the Divine Mother enter the Palace of the Heart. Visualize her sitting in the very center of the Lotus of your Heart and removing your pain and releasing all the dross. Feel your heart warm up in her presence. Ask her to bring you solace. Ask her to heal and console all aspects of your personality.

I would like to invoke other aspects of the Divine Mother to be present in the healing process. I invite the Presence of Mother Mary, Goddess Hecate, Pele, Athena, Quan Yin, and Isis to the Palace of the Heart. Watch each Presence graciously enter into the Palace of the Heart and take their seats inside the Lotus of your Heart. Continue to focus on the healing in your physical body as energy moves up the left side of your body to the top of your shoulder and down from the top of your head.

The Palace of the Heart is the hub of your Earthly and Heavenly bodies. To bring forth a healing and to manifest a reality, you can come to the Palace of the Heart. Visualize yourself seated inside the Lotus of the heart. The Great Lotus of the heart has twelve petals. Four petals represent the Feminine, four petals represent the Masculine and four petals represent the Child. This twelve petaled Lotus represents the Trinity of Father, Mother and Child. This Trinity is the complete Life-giving Force for your reality. The collective consciousness of humankind experiences the Trinity in the act of Creation which leads to the birthing of the Child. The cycle continues in regeneration, reproduction, and rebirthing.

Visualize the Lotus of the Heart expand in size. Step onto the petals and go to the golden center and seat yourself there facing the Divine Mother. Other aspects of Divine Mother are seated around you. Visualize your favorite Deities and Masters arriving to sit with you. Begin with the feminine deities who represent the Creative Force. Visualize them coming into this Great Hall which emanates Rose Pink and walk to the center stage, stepping up and seating themselves on the petals. Visualize that there are seats available for each of them around the outer petals and in the center of the lotus around you. Visualize yourself seated in the very center and bless the Presence of each Mother Aspect and commune with each one from your heart to theirs. Speak of your needs, your desires, your intentions, and ask each one for a healing. Be still and pause for a moment.

WE CALL FORTH THE ANGELIC FORCES OF THE FOUR DIRECTIONS

The Angelic Forces of Michael, Uriel, Gabriel and Rafael are now invited to take their positions around you. Michael stands behind you in the South, Uriel in front of you in the North, Rafael to your right in the East and Gabriel to your left in the West. Michael is sending you the Light of Divine Will and Divine Power in the color of Aquamarine-Blue. Uriel is sending you the Yellow Ray of Wisdom and Inner Light which illumines the Heart-Core of God-Source. Gabriel is sending you the Emerald Green Healing Light, the Light of Manifestation. Rafael sends you the Golden Pink Light of Healing and Love.

These Four Angelic Forces create a Cocoon of Light around you inside the Lotus of the Heart. From the mixing of the Blue Light of Divine Will and Power, the Yellow Light of Inner Light and Wisdom, the Emerald Green Healing Light, and the Golden Pink Healing Light of Love, a Bubble of Joy is created all around you in the Lotus. This Joy Bubble emanates a Golden Yellow color in every direction.

GODDESS HECATE

I call to the Presence of Goddess Hecate to begin to accelerate the healing process for you. As the Feminine Deity who holds the leash over Darkness, she is a symbol of Power and Might. Her presence on Earth is needed at this present moment for ending the duality and returning to Unity. Bless her presence as she too takes her seat on one of the petals of the Lotus and commune with her, giving her love and inviting her to heal and guide you. Ask Hecate for the removal of the cords and the release of karmic entanglements between your soul and the soul of your Twin Flame. Ask her to relieve you in all your Five Body Systems from the pain of separation and the dross of eons of lifetimes of betrayal, abandonment and rejection. Ask her to bring all the pain and the scars to the surface of your being. Now call the four Angelic Forces of Gabriel, Uriel, Rafael, and Michael. They can heal the pain, remove the scar, clear the grooves and bring you back to wholeness, health, Oneness and joy.

GODDESS PELE

I now call to the Presence of Goddess Pele, the Goddess of Fire and Volcanoes, the Guardian of Fire. In the Fire of Transmutation, she burns all that no longer serves you. Sit with Goddess Pele, ask her for the removal of dross, the burning of the deep rooted fears and pain of failure, rejection, and all unfinished business; releasing the pain from all the lifetimes filled with fear, disappointment and betrayal. I now ask four aspects of the Divine Mother; Hecate, Pele, Mother Mary, and Quan Yin to intercede on your behalf. Their intercession would be to stand before the Throne of the Undifferentiated Source, and invoke the Pure White Light to heal you and bring all aspects and fragments of your soul to health and wholeness. A Pillar of Light is forming above your head from the Heart-Core of the Undifferentiated Source. A shower of Pure White Light is pouring down, creating a Pillar of Light which illumines the Lotus. You and the four forms of the Divine Mother are seated inside.

TEMPLATE OF PERFECTED HEALTH AND WHOLENESS

On behalf of your soul, your spirit, your mind, your heart, your body, your emotions and all aspects of your personality, I ask for the downloading of the Template for the Original Blueprint of health and wholeness. I ask this Blueprint to be downloaded into your DNA structure and the Template to be established in your conscious and unconscious self. Every particle of your being, every aspect of your personality and every fragment of your soul is now receiving this healing. Take a deep breath.

I especially ask that your Feminine and Masculine Aspects come forth and unite in Oneness under the shower of this Light. They receive the Divine Template and come to wholeness. The Divine Blueprint of Wholeness is lodged in place. Divine Wholeness is re-established in all aspects of your personality, all fragments of your soul; manifesting health, wholeness and well-being throughout your entire being in your Five Body System. Receive, embody and imbue this Divine Blueprint. Take a deep breath.

I ask the Throne of Undifferentiated Source for the restoration of complete healing and wholeness. I ask for the removal of all scars, all grooves, and all damage inflicted upon your being throughout the eons of time in various physical incarnations. Breathe deeply and pause for a moment.

REJUVENATION

I call upon the Elemental Beings responsible for the upkeep of your physical body. The healing is now focused on the physical body for the reversal of the body clock. The rejuvenation of the body may begin now. I ask that all organs of your body be restored to optimum health with the help of the Elementals. The Life Force which moves through your body is brought to its optimal perfection, infusing every cell, every molecule, every atom, and every iota of your being. We are restoring the DNA structure to its Original Perfection. Breathe this healing essence into your organs, tissues, muscles and blood circulatory system. Visualize that this Light removes all cobwebs, all dross, all pain, and all memories of struggle, fear, loneliness and separation. Take a deep breath and pause as this healing is administered.

Repeat this exercise daily for twenty-two days or the entire month for optimum results and call upon my presence to shower you with my love. I am here at your service.

I am your very own Metatron. So it is.

CHAPTER VIII

PARAMATMAN LIGHT

In this beautiful invocational decree, Metatron teaches us to call the Light from its highest and purest source, the Paramatman. Paramatman is a Sanskrit word meaning "beyond-Atman". Atman is the self-realized soul. Such a soul has reached the point of Oneness yet remains cognizant of duality. Paramatman Light is completely beyond duality.

Reciting invocational decrees and Mantras like this one will help awaken us to the ultimate Light, beyond duality of this density, which is our true Source. Through the Light of Paramatman, our Atman Self can be activated. The Light of Paramatman is like the breath of Spirit which is blown into our soul to bring us back to life; a life filled with love from our Supreme Self to connect our Higher Self to us. Once fully connected, we live life without fears, without loneliness and without separation.

The Source in non-form, or non-manifest, is Undifferentiated Source and the Light which illuminates it is Pure White Light or Paramatman Light.

This is a great invocation and a powerful mantra. Repeat it at all times, in all places and share it with others who wish to accelerate themselves on the Path of Spiritual Enlightenment.

DESCENT OF PARAMATMAN LIGHT

Beloveds of my own heart, I am Metatron. Take a deep breath with me.

When we focus on clearing and cleansing Earth we will be able to restore it to the pure state of the original Divine Plan. This is achieved by going beyond form or beyond what has become differentiated. We can do this by taking the Five Elements back to their state of purity before differentiation. This will not only bring back the original state of purity but the original state of power to the Five Elements – Earth, Water, Fire, Air and Ether.

To accomplish the task we go to Paramatman Light in the heart-core of the Ether at the source of all things. The beauty of this process is that you are all the Light and the spirit of Paramatman. At present you are incarnated on Earth in a physical body of matter which has forgotten its existence in spirit as spirit. The ultimate goal is to help this body of physical matter to remember that it is the spirit of Paramatman

To reach this goal, we will have to accomplish a dual task. One segment is to Spiritize Matter, the other to Materialize Spirit. The Light of Paramatman will Spiritize Matter, and the Presence of the I Am will Materialize Spirit. Matter must be spiritized in order to return to its original Divine Self as spirit. Spirit needs to be materialized in order to bring its Light and Presence to this realm of matter and density. When you embody the I Am and connect to the Light of Paramatman, you become the catalyst for accomplishing this dual action.

At the level of Paramatman, there is no separation between form and non-form; matter and spirit. Pure Beingness is all there is. One aspect of Pure Beingness has taken form and accepted duality and the other aspect is sitting in the great, great silence, experiencing itself immersed in nothingness.

I ask of you to start repeating these mantras, invocations and intentions as many times a day and night as you can. Fall asleep with it. Wake up with it. In this way you can receive and embody the Paramatman Light.

Say each line three times. Three is the number for Creation. The Creative Force moves through you when you repeat each sentence. The energy of your intention is then set into creative motion.

Even if you do not recite the entire mantra fully during each repetition, it is best to recite each sentence three times. The first sentence alone is a powerful, potent and empowering mantra which opens you to receive and transmit greater Light and power.

Mantra for the Descent of Paramatman Light

In the name of the I Am That I Am
From the point of Light within the heart core of the Undifferentiated Source
I declare my Light on Earth.

The Light of the Paramatman I am.
I now declare the Paramatman Light through my body onto the Earth.
I command my body to receive this Light.
I command the Earth to receive this Light.
I command this Light to enter all souls.
I command all souls to receive this Light.

The Light of the Paramatman I Am.
The Life of the Paramatman I Am.
The Love of the Paramatman I Am.
The Spirit of the Paramatman I Am.

Paramatman Light I Am.
Paramatman Life I Am.
Paramatman Love I Am.
Paramatman Spirit I Am.

In the name of the I Am That I Am
From the point of Light within the heart core of the Undifferentiated Source
I declare my Light on Earth.

In the name of the Paramatman Light, I hold you in my own heart.
I ask for the grace and power of the Creation and the Creative Force of
The Divine Mother to bless and engulf you, from eternity to eternity.

I am your father, Metatron. So it is. It is done. Amen.

CHAPTER IX

ALCHEMY OF HEALING, PROTECTION AND MANIFESTATION

September is the time of Fall Equinox. Living in the third dimensional realm we are bound by time, space, polarity and density. All this makes the process of manifestation slow and difficult. The analogy of acceleration when using a microwave oven instead of a conventional oven is one way to understand how this grid can accelerate the process of manifestation. This exercise is also powerful for healing and protection. Many beings of Light offer their love and support in helping us heal and repel negativity. You may experience profound tingling and electrical energy surges within the body when performing this exercise.

Do this meditation throughout the month. Place greater focus and intent on the three days of Fall Equinox, the 19th, 20th and 21st, as these are important energy days, for greater healing and manifestation of abundance and peace.

Through this grid, Metatron is offering us an opportunity to be our own alchemist. Call upon Metatron to intercede on your behalf in creating greater alchemy for accelerating time and manifesting the objects of your desires. He is indeed a great alchemist.

In eternal love and in gratitude, I ask for blessings from the Masters for an abundant month and a joyful Fall Equinox.

GRID FOR HEALING, PROTECTION AND MANIFESTATION

Beloveds of my own heart, I am Metatron, El-Shaddai. Take a deep breath with me.

I would like to create a Grid of Protection and Healing around your body. To reach greater acceleration on your path to Enlightenment, you need to heal and empower yourself. To maintain a state of health and wholeness at all times, you need protection. This Grid of Light will become an important tool to achieve both. It can lighten your load of pain and dross as well as empower and protect you from harm. Then you can focus on greater acceleration of the manifestation process.

In this Grid of Light, we will work with two triangles. One will be a Triangle for Healing and the other a Triangle for Empowerment and for Protection. The Healing Triangle will emanate Green healing energies. The Protection Triangle will emanate Blue energies of empowerment.

The Green Healing Triangle will have three layers; a Citron-Green, an Emerald-Green and a Deep Dark Jade-Green for healing the mind, emotions and the body respectively. The Citron-Green is the Ray of Mental Clarity. The Emerald-Green is the Ray of Truth and Hope for the overall purging and healing of the emotional body. The Deep Dark Jade-Green is directly related to the healing of the physical body and the physical environment. This Deep Dark Jade-Green is also a connection to Earth and material things, including financial abundance and manifestation of material possessions. Archangel Raphael, Mother Mary and Quan Yin stand at the three points of this Green Triangle. They are beaming Green healing energy to you.

Intermingled with the Green Healing Triangle is the Blue Triangle of Empowerment and Protection. There are three layers of protection in three colors from the energies of The Blue Ray. The first layer is a Deep Dark Nile-Blue color which brings the power to protect you from all negativity. The presence of negativity in your energy field can lower your vibration and dis-empower you. This Deep Nile-Blue color is similar to the color of the sky at night. Its purpose and focus is to bring energy from the higher realms to the lower realms and release the negativity from your body and being. It will promote physical body clearing. The second layer is a Medium Blue Light, the color of chrysocolla stones (a little darker than turquoise). This will bring power to your etheric body, with special focus on the area of your Solar Plexus. It will also provide an emotional body clearing. Chrysocolla is a stone which vibrates to both the energies and qualities of turquoise and of lapis. Turquoise protects you from negative energies while lapis repels negativity. The Energetic power of chrysocolla provides both characteristics and brings the combined forces of both to your aid. The third layer is a transparent Aquamarine-Blue energy. Aquamarine-Blue is the energy for Divine Power and Mercy for this New Golden Age; it directs your attention to focus on your Divine Power and connects you to the Source of Divine Power. Archangel Michael, Archangel Uriel and Archangel Metatron stand at the three points of the Blue Triangle.

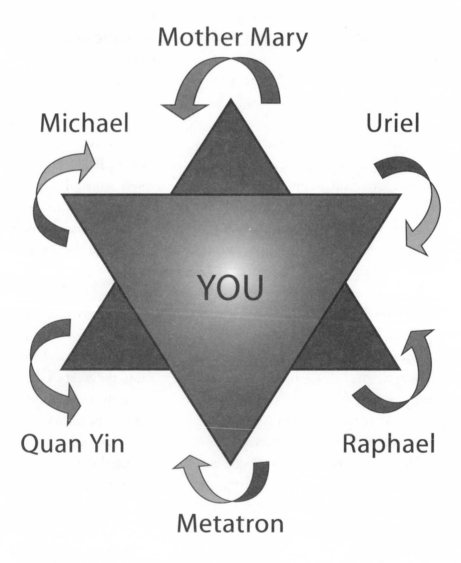

If you are unable to fully visualize the exact range of colors as explained here, do not be concerned, as the Masters are fully aware of your needs. They will administer the exact range of colors that are most beneficial for you. The Angels and Masters will work with you on this Grid and all you need to do is to call and ask for their guidance and assistance. They begin by beaming the three lights of the Blue Ray to you, protecting and guarding you from penetration of negativity from any external source and transmuting the negativity from within you. They will also assist in the process of empowering you to manifest your goals at an accelerated rate.

Envision that you are standing at the center of these two triangles which make a six pointed star. One triangle is emanating Blue Light to you and the other Green Light. Visualize Archangels Michael, Uriel and Metatron standing at the points of the Blue Triangle. Archangel Raphael, Mother Mary and Lady Quan Yin are standing at the points of the Green Triangle. A Shaft of Light is beaming down at the center where you stand.

This Shaft of Light is coming down from the Presence of the I Am That I Am. Reaching to your Crown Chakra, it moves through your head down to your spinal column to the base of your spine. Then it moves down from the base of your spine to reach to the crust of the Earth and on to the core of the Earth. Through you as the catalyst, the Shaft of Pure Light of the I Am That I Am moves from the thirteenth dimension of reality and reaches to the heart-core of Earth. It makes the Heavenly aspects of the Father energies, and the Earthly aspects of the Mother energies unite in Oneness through the medium of your own body.

Envision that each triangle spins around you, one moving clockwise, the other counter-clockwise. The Green Healing Triangle is bringing energy into your body and is therefore spinning clockwise. The Blue Triangle of Empowerment and Protection is releasing lower vibrational energies from your body. It is repelling all energies which lower the Light held within your physical, emotional and mental bodies. Therefore, the Blue Triangle is rotating counter-clockwise.

Feel the energy move through your body. You may feel waves of energy, heat or coolness move up and down your body. You may have a tingling sensation, see or sense the profusion of lights. Breathe deeply and feel the two triangles spin around you. The spin becomes faster. Begin to inhale deep long breaths and exhale deep slow breaths.

Imagine, as the energy moves to spin faster around you, it begins to form two Spheres of Light around your body. These Spheres spin emanating beams of Light in opposite directions, one emanating Green Light and the other Blue Light. The Spheres expand in size to become great Balls of Light around your entire body. The healing energies are absorbed through the Sphere moving clockwise. Negativity is released from your body through the Sphere moving counter-clockwise. The Spheres spin faster until your entire body begins to vibrate the Healing-Protection Energies of the Blue and Green Lights. Your body begins to absorb and respond to the energies of healing, power and protection. All that needs to be released from your body is now transmuted and returned to Pure Light. All that needs to be brought to your body is now retrieved from the Pure Light and brought to you. Each time you repeat this exercise, a new layer of release and empowerment is administered.

The three layers of Green mix with the three layers of Blue. Blue-Green Light of Healing, Power and Protection begin to emanate within and around you inside the two Spheres. When the two Spheres reach their optimum spin level, the Blue for Empowerment and Protection merges with the Green for Manifestation. The outcome will turn the entire Double Sphere into Pure Light. At that point everything implodes into Light. Then it explodes outward moving to the edges of the Double Spheres. Then once again the Light turns inward to go back to the center to implode. With each repetition another layer of dross is released.

The process of repeating the implosion-explosion will bring your intentions and the object of your desires into manifest form, blessed by the Presence of the I Am That I Am, embodied and imbued with the essence of Pure Light. Do this for three full rounds. At that point the exercise is complete. Then you may sit in peace, harmony, bliss and feel the joy of knowing that you have fully accomplished your task.

The Pure Light of the I Am That I Am will energize you and give you the strength and the stamina, the willpower and the Life Force which you need to accomplish all tasks; from mundane to sublime. Visualize this healing and Protection Grid every night before you fall asleep and every morning as you rise.

In addition to healing and protection, you can use this grid as a manifestation tool. Place whatever you wish to manifest in the center of this grid and spin the two triangles in the way I have described around that object. It can be an idea or an object which you would like to manifest, or a thought or an emotion you would like to release. Place that thought-form, object, or emotion in the center of this grid and begin to spin the two triangles around it. Envision and feel the spin of the two triangles. Begin to spin faster and state your intentions as you spin. Visualize manifesting all your desires in this way. Think of what you desire to see and experience in the course of the year ahead. State those intentions by mentioning them in full detail. For example, you can say,

"I wish to manifest this project — state it in detail — in the most accelerated speed." Or say, *"I desire to clear my life of all unnecessary events, release negativity, bring healing to myself and manifest all that I need to move on to serve the Light. I ask to be supported by the Light."*

If you wish to do both, you may combine the two intentions together. For example, imagine that you hold the object of your desires in your hands or hold the thought or idea for what you desire to manifest in your mind and visualize yourself spin inside the two triangles. Visualize that the energy of the spin is reaching full force. The triangles begin to emit Light and become spherical. In an instant they will begin to move into an implosion/explosion. With the explosion, Pure Light begins to emanate from the core of your being in every direction. The two Spheres begin to expand in size to encompass your entire body.

Now sit in the Pure Light. Let your mind be absorbed in the acceptance that your desires have been completely fulfilled. Command the Angelic Forces of Light who work with you to illuminate your Personal Grid with this intention. They will then begin building the Grid to illuminate the ultimate reality which will hold this intention. They will retrieve the Original Blueprint for the design and the idea for your intention from the Mind of God. This idea or thought-form which has occurred to you has its origin within the Mind of God. That Original Divine Blueprint holds all possible thoughts and actions which are divinely ordained.

Command your Angelic Forces of Light and say, *"I now command my Guardian Angels of Light to retrieve the Divine Blueprint from the Mind of God and to illuminate my Personal Body Grid with it."* In this way you align your mind with the Divine Mind and your own Will with the Divine Will. Such a Divine Plan will fully satisfy your personality aspects, your mind and your emotions. It will also satisfy your soul and the Divine Mission that your soul has come to fulfill in this lifetime.

When you perform this exercise for twenty-two consecutive days without a break, the manifestation power, the healing, the cleansing and the protection will become part of your Personal Light Grid. As a result you will be able to call forth its powers. After the first twenty-two day phase you can move on to make a new grid with new intentions. When you repeat the exercise, the visualization can come to you in an instant and the process accelerated as you visualize it to turn into Pure Light.

In the third dimension of reality, time and space move slower than in the fifth dimension where thoughts are manifested instantaneously. This grid will help you turn your thoughts into actions at a faster pace. Your focus, your desire to succeed and your clarity of intent all play a role in the acceleration process. However, bear in mind that you are working in a high-density third dimensional realm where the manifestation process has been slowed down. You need to accelerate time and space before things can manifest. By spinning this grid, you can accelerate the future to come closer to this now moment. How fast that future can come to this now moment depends on how fast the density can be moved. Your greater focus, your intense desire and your perseverance can all add up to greater results.

The principles act similar to the concept of a microwave oven. Microwave energy spins the molecules of food to jump up and down creating heat. When you place the cold or uncooked food inside of the microwave oven it cooks much faster than conventional methods of cooking. The same concept can be applied with this grid. Imagine wanting to do something that would take a long time to accomplish, if you were letting time and space take its normal course for its manifestation. Then you decide, *"I want to manifest this in the highest possible accelerated speed. I plan to move on to serve the Light, and I desire to be supported by the Light."* Put that object, thought-form or emotion inside of the grid, and say, *"accelerate it to the best of the ability of time and space in compliance with the Divine Plan."* The Divine Plan can give it to you in an instant, yet since you live in the third dimensional reality, you may have to wait for a while longer before you see results. Meanwhile, continue to accelerate the result by repeating this exercise to help time and space catch up with your intentions faster.

The grid can assimilate turning your intention into Microwave Rays of Light. If an event were to take three years to accomplish, with this grid it can be done in three months. This is the alchemical benefit of the grid. If time and space were to comply with your needs and move from solid density to flowing liquidity, then the object of your desires could come to you in a matter of seconds, minutes, days, weeks, rather than years and decades. Take a deep breath.

This Grid of Light for Healing and Manifestation is imbued with the alchemy of fifth dimensional energies. In the fifth dimension, thoughts manifest as objects in a matter of seconds. You can manifest things by simply putting out the intention, creating a triangle of Light around it, spinning the triangle into a sphere and letting the sphere turn into Pure Light. The entire process happens instantaneously. In the fifth dimension you may think, *"I am hungry, I want an apple,"* and an apple appears in your hand, fresh and filled with Life Force Energy. Even in the fourth dimensional realm you can replicate the manifestation process with much greater ease than you can in the third dimension.

By knowing the principals and alchemical secrets which can turn base metal into gold, you can turn the object of your desires into manifest form, or turn a thought-form into the object of your desires. You can turn thoughts into tangible objects. This exercise, once mastered, can bring you the alchemy of turning base metal into gold.

I leave you now. I hold you in my own heart. I will continue to give you healing through this grid.

I am your very own Metatron, El-Shaddai. So it is.

"I offer myself in service to the Lords of Light and ask to be fully immersed in their energies."
Metatron

CHAPTER X

LORDS OF LIGHT AND THE CREATIVE FORCE

Metatron has requested that we call upon Goddess Hecate to help us release the darkness from within us and to transmute the dross from our personal and planetary environment. Her strength in protecting us from negativity and her ability to transmute dross should always be our solace. We must call upon her for assistance often. Metatron stresses the importance of raising the vibrational force-field of the planet through the Feminine Energy and the Creative Force of the Mother Divine. At this present juncture we can greatly benefit from invoking the Divine Mother to become an active guiding force in our lives, especially in her aspect as Goddess Hecate. Metatron also talks about the importance of calling upon Athena whose wisdom as a warrior Goddess of Justice is sorely needed at this present time. Goddess Liberty and Victory are called to Liberate humankind from the dross of pain and make us Victorious in Light.

I wish you great joy in uniting your energies with that of the Divine Mother and pray that she will bless you with great prosperity, love, Light, abundance and great success in all your endeavors.

CLEARING ENERGY BODIES

Beloveds of my own heart, I am Metatron, El-Shaddai.

Take a deep breath with me and focus your energy in the center of your Heart Chakra.

The Earth and all souls have finally reached a point of awareness where we can finally begin to release the Duality and return to Unity. It is now time for the union of Light and Dark. Once Light and Dark merge into each other, we can move from the duality of separation to the unity of Oneness. As beacons of Light and the emissaries of the Lords of Light, you can accelerate this process for yourself and for Earth. My intention is to assist you to accomplish this task. To this end I ask you to continuously Say,

"I call forth the Presence of the Lords of Light to take over the guardianship of Earth and all souls. I especially ask for their intercession on my behalf and their intervention in my life. I offer myself in service to the Lords of Light and ask to be

fully immersed in their energies. In their name I ask for whatever lower vibrations and darkness remains within and around me to be released now. I am free from all darkness. My life is accelerated in service to Light under the guardianship of the Lords of Light."

Through this statement you acknowledge the darkness which has existed in your lives and in your environment, yet you call upon the Forces of Light as your protector. Acknowledging the existence of a negative force and your focused intent to release it, will accelerate the process; ignoring or denying its existence will prolong your agony and delay your growth. Once addressed, delays, distractions, fears, anger and other negative emotions can be avoided. Through the above statement, you are asking the Lords of Light to take charge and become the long awaited leaders and Guardians of Earth and your lives.

Ask the Masters of Light in the entourage of Christ Maitreya to intercede on your behalf. Remember that great Light and guidance is available to clear your path from obstacles. All you need do is to ask. To help you clear yourself of all dross and darkness, I will give you a clearing exercise and invite the Presence of the Feminine Principle, the Divine Creative Force in her aspect as Goddess Hecate, to bring you her blessing. Call upon Hecate whenever you feel the need to release darkness from your life and when you feel stagnant. Light a red candle in her name and in her honor. Find a statue or picture of her and place it at a high point in your home or office to allow her to look over you from above. Keep the red candle lit near her at all times. Hecate should be honored during all phases of the moon, whether it is during the new moon phase, the full moon, waning or waxing. Honor Goddess Hecate wherever the moon is, and honor her vigorously during the month of October which denotes entry into the dark season of the year in the Northern Hemisphere and exit from the dark season in the Southern. Normal practice is to pay respect to Goddess Aphrodite during the new and waxing moon, Goddess Celina during full moon and Goddess Hecate during the waning moon, yet you can honor and pay tribute to Hecate during all phases of the moon. She will return your loving tribute by interceding on your behalf. Honor her in the spring as a Maiden and in the fall as a wise woman. Both aspects can denote rebirthing; the spring of a new life or the death of an old, prior to rebirthing of another. Let this be a new beginning and let go of all your fears.

Now we will begin to clear and cleanse all your energy bodies. Focus your attention on your body as I begin to clear each layer of your energy body. The clearing will be performed while Brilliant Light moves down a cylinder, pushing down and out all dross and negativity from the top of your body to the bottom of your feet. The technique we use is much like moving the disc or blade of a coffee filter inside the glass jar of a coffee press. In this case, the blade is made of Light and the glass jar is a large cylinder of Light. The blade of Light moves down inside the Cylinder pushing the dross out of your body, releasing it from the bottom of your feet into the crust of the Earth for transmutation.

Physical Body Clearing

We will start with the physical body. You are now standing inside the Cylinder of Light of the I Am That I Am. The Pure White Light of the Undifferentiated Source is pouring into the Cylinder of Light, moving down through the Presence of the I Am That I Am and reaching further down to you. The Light begins to clear pollution and dross of this and many other lifetimes from your body. Visualize the Light moving from the top of your head all the way down your body to the bottom of your feet. Clearing the pollution and dross out of your body, the Light moves through the crust of the Earth and into the core.

The energies of the Undifferentiated Source, God in non-manifest form, moves down to become manifest as the I Am That I Am. Then the combined forces of God in non-form, as super consciousness and God in Form, as individualized consciousness, pour down to you and through you to Earth. From its crust to its core, the Earth too is cleansing itself from her dross through this exercise. You have become the catalyst to clear and cleanse Earth from her crust to her core. Take a deep breath.

Clearing of the Etheric Body

Now we will clear your etheric body and your auric field. Visualize that Pure White Light is pouring down to you from above. It moves from the top of your etheric body down inside the Cylinder of White Light. As the Blade of Light moves downward, it clears your etheric body. It goes down all the way to the crust of the Earth and to the core, completely clearing and cleansing all dross on its way down. Your etheric body is now extending and expanding inside of the Cylinder of Pure White Light. Take a deep breath.

Clearing of the Emotional Body

We move now to the emotional body, the third energy body. We start at the Twelfth Chakra, where the I Am That I Am resides. Your Antakharana cord which is the Thread of Light connecting you to that realm is now illuminated. The intention is to imbue and embody purity of essence, clarity of focus, wisdom, love, Light and the willingness to accomplish your Divine Mission. Visualize the Cylinder of Pure White Light as it moves downwards from the Presence of the I Am That I Am, clearing all levels as it moves down, chakra by chakra from above your emotional body to the crust of the Earth and finally to the core of the Earth. You are completely clearing your emotional body and restoring it to the perfection of the Original Plan. Take a deep breath.

Clearing of the Mental Body

We repeat the process for the fourth energy body, the Mental Body. Visualize Light pouring down inside the Cylinder of Pure White Light from the Presence of the I Am That I Am at the thirteenth dimension of reality. It pours down to the twelfth dimension of reality, eleventh dimension of reality, tenth dimension of reality, ninth dimension of reality, eighth dimension of reality, seventh dimension of reality, sixth dimension of reality, fifth dimension of reality, reaching to the soul at the Eighth Chakra in the fourth dimension of reality. Finally it moves to the third dimension of reality and enters into the crown, moving down through the Third Eye, Throat, Cosmic Heart, Heart, Seat of the Soul, Solar Plexus, Sacral Plexus, Root Chakra, thighs, knees, calves, ankles, feet, crust of the Earth and core of the Earth. A complete clearing will take place which allows the Mental Body to expand and extend and reach the edges of your Cylinder of Light. Your Mental Body is now fully merged into the Cylinder of Pure White Light of the I Am That I Am. Take a deep breath.

Clearing of the Spiritual Body

We now move to the fifth and last layer of Energy Body to clear and reconnect with your spiritual body. The spiritual body does not become contaminated. Therefore it only needs to be reconnected to the highest aspect and essence of your soul and to the chakras of your body. When fully connected, the soul will enter into the body and reside in the Chakra of the Seat of the Soul, located between your Heart Chakra and your Solar Plexus. To connect the soul to the highest throne of Light, we will take it to the ultimate essence of the God-Source or spirit of Oneness at the Throne of the Undifferentiated Source. We will begin by connecting the spiritual body through the antakharana, the thread of Light, through the I Am That I Am all the way to the Presence of the Undifferentiated Source.

The physical body is the vehicle for the Soul. The spiritual body is the vehicle for Spirit. For each of these five energy bodies to function at their best and be fully connected to their Source, they must first be cleared from their dross. The spiritual body must be reconnected to the physical body in the third dimension and to the Undifferentiated Source in the one hundred and eighth dimension. Then Spirit can move freely from one to the other and the Soul can occupy the body. When all lower bodies are cleared and united, then Soul and Spirit can be united. In this way the body is connected to Soul and Spirit. Without the soul, the body is just a vehicle much like a robot. Without the life giving force of Spirit the soul is unable to fully function. Think of the example where the body is a vase or jar, the soul is the flower which sits in the jar and the spirit is the life giving force that keeps the flower alive. All of these components are necessary, otherwise the flower will die and the jar will be empty. Body, soul and spirit, in union can begin moving forward, extending and expanding through all levels and dimensions of reality.

To bring the spirit of the Creative Force to all bodies of matter on Earth, you can begin to work with different aspects of the Divine Mother, the Feminine Principle of Creation. For example, Goddess Athena's wisdom and essence as a Warrior Goddess is sorely needed at this present juncture in Earth's evolution. We are also in need of the Goddess of Victory and Goddess of Liberty. Goddess of Victory has been victorious for over 200,000 years, Goddess of Liberty has been liberating humankind from the dross of fear for over 500,000 years and Goddess Athena has been the Warrior Goddess of all women, all soldiers and all teachers for a few thousand years.

Grid of Protection

From this moment on, call upon these Goddesses to walk with you. Walk with Goddess Athena standing behind you, Goddess of Victory standing to your left and Goddess of Liberty to your right in the formation of a triangle. Goddess Athena holds her sword above your head and her shield in front of your Solar Plexus. Visualize yourself encased inside the energy field of these three goddesses. Inside this triangle you are completely protected in their embrace. Take a deep breath.

Visualize this formation spinning around you. As this formation spins, the three points of the triangle also begin to spin. The spin becomes faster and faster, then the three points implode inside of you in the center. When this implosion happens, the power of Goddess of Victory, the freedom of Goddess of Liberty and the wisdom of Goddess Athena, enter into you and begin to reside within you.

Now visualize that Goddess Hecate is standing in front of you. She is holding a torch in each hand and is shining her Light upon your path. You walk behind her as a child who follows his mother. She will show you the way and illuminate the path ahead to protect you from all harm and accelerate you on the path of Light.

Spin this Grid every night before you fall asleep and every morning as you arise. Visualize this Protection Grid of Light around you all the time. I pray that your success will be great, your path clear of obstacles, your ride smooth and your joy boundless.

I hold you in my own heart with great love.

I am your very own Metatron, so it is.

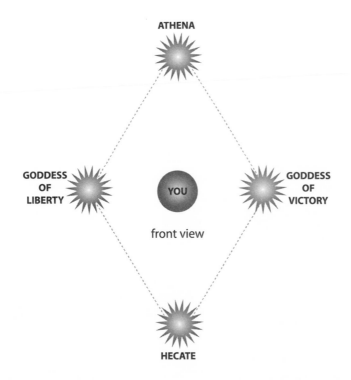

Clearing Energy Bodies and Grid of Protection

- Light a red candle to invoke Divine Mother and honor her presence in your life by invoking Goddess Hecate to spread her power, passion and protection over you.

- Purify your Five Body System by visualizing a blade of Light running through the five layers:

- Clear the physical body

- Clear the etheric body

- Clear the emotional body

- Clear the mental body

- Clear the spiritual body

- Visualize yourself standing at the center of a triangle inside the formation of a Grid of Light.

- Goddess of Victory is to your left, Goddess of Liberty to your right, and Goddess Athena is behind you with her sword above your head and her shield held in front of your body.

- Spin the three points of the triangle until they implode into you at the center.

- Visualize yourself fully immersed in Oneness with Athena, Victory and Liberty.

- Visualize yourself standing behind Goddess Hecate as she walks ahead of you. In each hand she points a torch of Light to illuminate your path, remove all obstacles, darkness and fear from your path.

Do the entire exercise for twenty-two days. Visualize yourself at all times immersed in the energy of these four powerful Goddesses. Remind yourself of this Grid of Light every morning, every evening and during the day whenever you desire greater protection and acceleration to success and joy.

CHAPTER XI

PROTECTION AND TRANSMUTATION

Metatron is offering us a Grid of Light for protection from the negative and lower vibrational energies coming to the surface at both personal and planetary levels. He speaks about the release of anger from the body of the planet and from the consciousness of all souls. His intention is to help us realize that we may be experiencing more than our personal share of anger because as Light-workers it is our job to transmute lower vibrational frequencies on behalf of Earth and all souls. He is also offering to help release these energies from Earth and the collective consciousness of humankind. Bathe in the love from the four Angelic Forces called to present this Grid of Light. Use this Grid whenever you feel out of sorts. It will shift the energies to break up the negativity and loosen up the dross from around you and clear your personal energy bodies. It will assist in protecting you from harm and lower vibrational forces. The release of dross and anger, which has been with us for many lifetimes, will lighten our load and allow us to fill our hearts with greater joy and happiness.

As mentioned before, the Great Silent Watcher is a great being who is responsible for the creation of our planet and the entire solar system. She is like a God-Mother to us and our planet. Metatron has invoked her presence to beam a Bubble of Turquoise-Blue Light to surround us and to protect us from the turbulent energies of this present time. The four angelic forces of Michael, Gabriel, Uriel and Raphael are the Guardians of the Four Directions and Great Beings who stand at the Throne of God. Metatron is calling them to come to our assistance and protection during these times of rapid planetary changes. These changes are shifting the focus of our planet and the collective consciousness of all souls from Darkness to Light. This is indeed the case, even though it may seem otherwise from the outward appearance of current events; the natural disasters, man-made conflicts, wars and diseases. It pays to be patient with ourselves, our loved ones and our environment and know this is meant to bring greater good for humankind as well as Mother Earth.

I wish you a great journey on the path of joy. May God speed you in releasing all fear, anger and pain.

GRID OF LIGHT FOR RELEASE OF ANGER, FEAR, PAIN AND STRUGGLE

Beloveds of my own heart, I am Metatron.

Presently, the energies of Earth have a tendency to shift suddenly from one moment to the next. This can cause those with sensitive constitutions to experience energies of dross, anger, pain and fear coming unexpectedly to the surface. The experience may be at subconscious levels. You may be led to believe that it is your own personal circumstances that cause your moods to change. You may not realize that part of what you experience is externally induced and relates to the pain and the dross that is being released on behalf of Earth and the consciousness of all souls. Those of you who are higher initiates on the Path of Light are taking on this dross to transmute it on behalf of Earth and others. These energies, even though externally induced, are recalibrated through your own physical bodies for transmutation. They move through your physical body and are released from the atmosphere of Earth and the consciousness of souls. This is your service to the Light. For this reason I would like to offer you a Grid of Light to lighten your load during this time and help you cope with the energies of anger coming to the surface of Earth and the consciousness of humankind.

You may experience this anger as if it appears from nowhere, causing you emotional upheaval, grief, struggle, fear and pain. This Grid of Light will release the anger from your bodies and prevent any external lower vibrational energy from penetrating your body and your being. When you use this Grid, you may not be aware of the anger at all but it will nevertheless continue to assist with the transmutational process, from your personal as well as global point of view. Its benefits are to free you from many lifetimes of accumulated anger, fear and pain and free the Earth from carrying the pain of Humanity in her atmosphere and her auric field. Lightening the load will free all souls and the planet, leaving you all in a much greater state of harmony and peace. Once these energies are released, peace will follow and a state of harmony and calm will be induced.

Meditation for the Release of Anger, Fear, Pain and Struggle

Visualize standing in the center of a circle with the Angelic Forces of the Four Directions forming a circle around you. Archangel Uriel is standing in the direction of North, directly facing you. Archangel Michael is standing in the direction of South, directly behind you. Archangel Rafael is to your right in the direction of East, and Archangel Gabriel is to your left in the direction of West. Archangel Uriel will be beaming the Inner Light in the color of Yellow from his heart and from the palms of his upraised hands. Archangel Rafael is sending you the Pink Light of Divine Love from the heart and palms of the hands. Archangel Michael is beaming the Ray of Compassion and Mercy in the color of Aquamarine-Blue. Archangel Gabriel is beaming the Healing Light in the color of Emerald-Green.

The Great Silent Watcher, a great being of love and Light, is hovering above this entire Grid. From the space of her heart, she is sending a Bubble of Light in the color of Turquoise-Blue. This bubble forms around you and the four Archangels. The energy substance of this Bubble holds the texture and qualities of the precious stone Turquoise within it. Turquoise removes negative energies from the physical body, the emotional body and the mental body. It prevents anger, pain, jealousy, envy, fear, worry, and panic, from penetrating into your being. It protects you from the external elements that cause anger and discomfort.

Visualize yourself at the center of this Grid of Light with the four Angelic Forces all around you, each sending you the Light of their respective Ray and the qualities that they carry. Lower vibrational energies will now come to the surface to be transmuted. For the transmutation of these energies, I now call forth an inferno of the Violet Flame to create a cylinder of Violet Light around you. Visualize Violet Light spiraling from the base of your feet upward, winding its way all around you, spiraling counterclockwise and reaching to the top of your head. A cylinder of Purple Light is now forming around you which will encompass your entire body. This cylinder is about five feet wide and extends from the ground all the way to the top of your head and further up, releasing all lower energies which come to the surface. The spiraling whirlwind of the Violet Flame moves upward and outward from the base of your feet to the top of your head and beyond. It only moves in one direction, up and out. Energies such as anger, fear, pain and dross are being pulled from your own body into the Violet Cylinder of Light and transmuted upward and outward away from your body. The spiraling Violet Flame is releasing pain and dross from your mental and emotional and physical body, freeing you from many lifetimes of pain, anger, hardship and struggle and helping you transmute what you pick up from the surface of Earth and the collective consciousness of humankind. Take a few deep breaths and continue to visualize this entire Grid of Light. Continue to keep this visualization and take a few deep long inhalations followed by slow long exhalations. Now I give you a mantra to repeat:

Mantra for Release of Anger, Fear, Pain and Struggle

In the Violet Light of Transmutation I stand
In the Turquoise Light of the Silent Watcher I Am
In the Blue Protective Light of Michael I Am
In the Pink Light of Rafael I Am
In the Yellow Light of Uriel I Am
In the Green Light of Gabriel I Am
I release all dross from all dimensions and realities
I offer this dross through the intercession of the Great Silent Watcher
For transmutation into Pure Light
The Brilliant White Light of Paramatman I Am
The White Light of Undifferentiated Source I Am
The Golden White Light of Ellah I Am
The Blue Light of God-Source I Am
The Gold Light of YHWH I Am
The Pure Light I Am
I Am That I Am
I Am, I Am, I Am
So it is.
It is done.
Amen.

Use this Grid for a twenty-two day period of time. It is best to do it consecutively, however, do not worry if you miss a day. Continue by adding the missed days at the end. Start this Grid while the present energies are coming forth to help protect you during this time of release. Repeat this exercise whenever you feel energies of anger, fear and pain come to the surface. These energies are accumulated through many lifetimes of pain, struggle, rejection, abandonment and betrayal. It is helpful to use this Grid, especially when you feel an onslaught of angry thoughts or emotions. After the first phase of clearing, you may use this Grid of Light whenever you feel the need. Ask the Great Silent Watcher and the Angelic Forces of Uriel, Rafael, Michael and Gabriel to continue to work on your body and being around the clock for the full release of all negativity and lower vibrations.

I hold you in my own heart, I Am Metatron.

"My Prayer is to love yourself enough to want
what is best for yourself and trust the world enough
to give it away again and again and again,
knowing it will come back to you tenfold,
a hundred fold, a thousand fold,
over and over again."
Goddess Hecate

CHAPTER XII

ABUNDANCE AND PROSPERITY

The Divine Mother has requested that we make an Abundance Magnification Grid of Light. Goddess Hecate offers this grid, invoking thirteen aspects of Divine Mother.

Magnification Grids are extremely powerful. There are three components to a Magnification Grid. The first is the candles. When charged, candles can carry the energy of a specific thing or a certain quality. The second is the crystals which magnify the intentions for the Grid and add acceleration. The third is the intercession of the Great Beings invoked to add their powerful energies to the Grid. In this Grid, we call upon thirteen mighty aspects of the Divine Mother. The sequence in this Candle Grid of Light is that the candles empower the crystals. The crystals magnify the intention for the grid and the power and might of the thirteen Goddesses further accelerate our intentions. The Divine Mother has decreed to provide for all our mundane needs, especially to bring financial prosperity and abundance through this grid.

DIVINE MOTHER ON ABUNDANCE AND PROSPERITY

My Children of Light, I am your Divine Mother.

I have called you because we are moving into accelerated energies of Light. This means you have a chance to use the force of this acceleration to gain momentum in all your endeavors. You can expand yourself physically as well as spiritually by surfing the tide of these energies. When you are fully contented and when the world offers you all you need in abundance, you have a much better chance to serve the Light. You can then allocate all your time and energy to fulfilling your Divine Mission. For as long as you struggle for survival, you are distracted from the real purpose of your incarnation, your soul purpose.

This is why I say to you; seriously and constantly ask for financial abundance and for physical empowerment to use in service to the Light. Keep asking for it until you are fully satisfied. Make it a mantra, on a moment to moment basis with every breath; ask for abundance and prosperity in your life. In joy and in gratitude, ask for all that you want. Ask for everything which makes your life easier, comfortable, enjoyable, healthier, wholesome, peaceful and harmonious.

When you do not expend your energy in struggling to survive you can be of much greater service to the Light, to the beloved Masters and to me, your Divine Mother.

When you become strong, powerful, healthy, whole and joyful, you can carry a much greater expanse of Light. You can be of greater assistance to the Masters. All the time, in all places, with your mind and your heart, seek to be better, greater, vaster, capable of absorbing Light and spreading that Light to all. Say,

"I am happy, I am joyful, I am grateful, I am peaceful, and I am harmonious with all Elements. I seek from all Elements, I seek from the Universe, I seek from the Masters, I seek from the Light, I seek from the Lords of Light, I seek from the Guardians of Light guidance and assistance for greater financial abundance; greater prosperity, greater resources, greater people in my service, greater output from the Five Elements; greater above and beyond expectation, greater above and beyond limitation. I seek from the unlimited resources; I seek from the unlimited potential of the Universe. I seek from the unlimited potential of the Throne of the Divine Mother, Throne of Undifferentiated Source, Throne of Paramatman Light, and Throne of Creation. I seek greater abundance; I seek above and beyond limitation. I seek and I call to me the unlimited resources of the Universe."

I seek greater abundance and prosperity from the Five Elements which are the building blocks of our Creation. I seek abundance and prosperity from the Universe, from the Masters, from the Light, from the Lords of Light and from the Guardians of Light. I seek and I shall be prosperous and abundant now and forever.

I ask all Divine Thrones and the Masters of Light to help me tap into the unlimited potential of the Universe and to widen the pathways for me to reach unlimited abundance, unlimited resources and unlimited power. I call to the unlimited potential of the vastness of the Universe and I magnetize it to myself. I merge into the Magnetic Force Field of the Feminine Principle and pull it to myself with every breath. I seek and I pull to myself greater and greater levels of magnetism for greater potential to pour down, greater ability to do more in service to the Light, greater momentum and greater acceleration in the evolution of my soul and in all worldly endeavors."

Call to the Divine Mother and Say,

"Let me be grounded, let me have my feet on the ground. Let me be in total surrender, accepting and knowing that my abundance is imminent. Help me get my footing; help me know where I am. Help me keep my eyes wide open, help me have my hands ready to receive, help me have my arms outstretched, help me have my arms strong. Teach me to be your Child of Light. Remind me that I am yours and you are mine. I offer my Light, my joy, my life and my all in service to you. I am Light, I am abundant, I am prosperous, I am harmonious, I am peaceful, I am joyful, and I am in Oneness with All That Is, for I Am All That Is."

Remember my children, it is a Universal Law; *"Ask and you shall receive."* When you are in need and you ask, the Universe is bound to come to your help. You may think that to ask for worldly things, for personal use, would be selfish and inappropriate, especially when you choose to be spiritual. You may have been lead to believe that because you choose to walk more steadily on the path of Spiritual Enlightenment; that you must ask for less. I tell you this is not true. You have every right to ask for everything and even more so because you are a spiritually awakened soul. As an awakened soul, you do more for Earth, Humanity and Light than the un-awakened souls. Therefore, more is to be offered to you by the Universe.

In the wise words of Mother Meera, a physically incarnate manifestation of Divine Mother on Earth at this present moment, *"Make it a habit to ask the Divine for everything."* www.mmdarshanamerica.com

For the resources to open up to you, you must first believe that you disserve it, that you are worthy to have the best that this world has to offer. Why should you be deprived? You have come to be the Light that shines upon this Earth and illumines the path for all souls. You are leading Earth and all souls to a greater future. You deserve to be treated to the utmost best of all the resources available on Earth. I ask you to call upon me, Your Divine Mother, for all things, absolutely all things and expect to have your needs met, your desires fulfilled and your life filled with Light, love and luxury. I am here by your side. I love you with all of my heart.

I am your Divine Mother.

CANDLE GRID FOR FINANCIAL ABUNDANCE

My Children of Light, I am Hecate.

In deference to my beloved Divine Mother, I give you a Candle Grid to bring you abundance and prosperity and to accelerate the process of manifestation. Through this Grid, I invite the energies of thirteen aspects of the Divine Mother to intercede on your behalf. Divine Mother would like you to receive all the assistance possible. I am inviting Goddess Hecate, Lady Quan Yin, Athena, Pele, Isis, Lady Liberty, Lady Victory, Lady Nada, Mother Mary as well as the four Hindu aspects of Divine Mother, Saraswati, Goddess of Knowledge and Wisdom, Lakshmi, Goddess of Material and Spiritual Abundance, Durga, Destroyer of Karma and Protector of Humankind and Kali, the Mother Goddess, Remover of Darkness from this Age known as the Age of Kali Yuga.

The thirteen Goddesses will be invited to imbue a candle with their own energies to protect you, guide you, teach you and accelerate you in your mundane worldly life and to accelerate and illuminate you on your spiritual path.

I am also bringing to you the alchemy of the energies of the Gold color, Red color and Black color. These three colors will be encapsulated in a red candle, a gold candle and a black candle.

The red candle is intended to connect you with the Earth energy and to bring you the abundance of Earth. Red represents the Life Force of Earth; it is also the Life Force of the human body and human being. The intention for the gold candle is to bring Life Force and the unlimited abundance of the Creative Force into your life. The intention for the black candle is to release and remove all the darkness.

The Red is for the Life Force of Earth, Gold for alchemical, attraction and magnetism to bring prosperity and abundance; the Life Force of the Heavenly Realms. Black is for the Force and the Power of Transmutation, for the release of darkness.

For instructions on how to draw your Candle Grid and how to energize it with your intentions, please refer to the diagram in the summary that follows.

I send you much love and much joy and much healing and prayers. And I promise you that monies and resources will manifest for you.

I hold you with great joy in my own heart. I thank you for all the love that you give to me. Buy a statue of Goddess Hecate and display it in a high position in your home or office. In this way I can look out for you from above. Put that statue on top of a red cloth. This will bring you acceleration by adding the Red Light of Creative Life Force to the environment.

I hold you in my heart with great joy; I am your Mother Hecate. Blessed be.

Summary and Instructions for Making the Candle Grid
Materials Needed
- Note: Large pillar candles are recommended but for your convenience, any size will work.
- One large Red Pillar Candle
- One large Gold Pillar Candle (Use Yellow if you can't find Gold)
- One large Black Pillar Candle

- 9 tea lights or white votives
- One 12" x 12" red, black or yellow poster board
- One blue or purple marker or pen
- One crystal piece, preferably a clear quartz cluster
- One piece of gold, (Gold coin, gold jewelry or gold colored coin)

You may copy or print the diagram shown here, or follow the directions below.

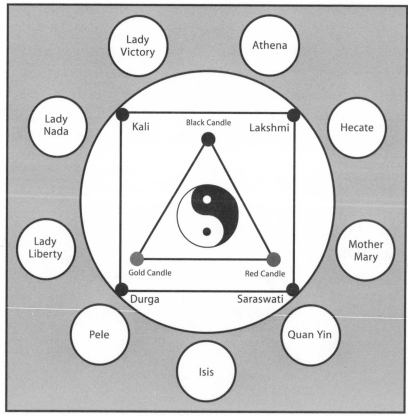

Yellow Poster Board

Directions for drawing your Candle Grid

1. Draw a large circle on the poster board.

2. Draw an equilateral triangle, with approximately 9" sides, inside the circle. The triangle should not touch the circle.

3. Draw a square with each corner touching the circle.

4. At the center of the poster board draw a circle approximately 2" in diameter.

5. Inside the small circle, draw the sign of infinity. Superimpose the Yin-Yang symbol over the sign of infinity by placing a dot in the center of each loop and coloring in one side of the Ying-Yang. Let the merging of the infinity and the sign of Ying-Yang, which is the male and female, the masculine and feminine polarities be merged into each other.

6. Place a mound of cinnamon over the two merged symbols. On top of the mound place a crystal cluster and a piece of gold. You can place a piece of gold jewelry, gold chain, a solid gold or a golden colored coin. Gold transmutes all negativity, the higher the karat, the higher the potency.

7. To charge your crystal cluster, hold the crystal up and Say,

"I invoke the Presence of Goddess Hecate, Lady Quan Yin, Athena, Pele, Isis, Lady Liberty, Lady Victory, Lady Nada, Mother Mary as well as the four Hindu aspects of Divine Mother, Saraswati, Goddess of Knowledge and Wisdom, Lakshmi, Goddess of Material and Spiritual Abundance, Durga, Destroyer of Karma and Protector of Humankind and Kali, the Mother

Goddess, Remover of Darkness from this Age known as the Age of Kali Yuga and I ask all aspects of the Divine Mother to charge the crystal with the energies of abundance and prosperity and to hold and magnify each intention placed into the Grid as I light each candle."

8. Sprinkle cinnamon around the entire large circle covering the line that you drew.

9. Place the red, gold and black candles at the 3 points of the triangle.

10. Write Saraswati, Durga, Lakshmi and Kali on the four corners of the square. Place 4 tea candles at each of the 4 points over the four names.

11. Mark 9 points equally spaced around the large circle. Make these points about 1" outside the large circle. Write the names of the Goddesses at each one of these 9 points. Write Hecate, Athena, Mother Mary, Quan Yin, Lady Nada, Lady Liberty, Lady Victory, Pele and Isis.

12. Place 9 tea candles at the name of each of the 9 Goddesses.

Lighting the Candle Grid

Start with the three large candles.

1. Pick up the black candle, hold it up and say,

"I call forth the transmutational forces of Heaven and Earth to remove all darkness from my life and my being. Release and remove all obstacles from my path of abundance and prosperity and accelerate the manifestation of all beneficial resources into my life and my hands." Place the black candle back on the grid and light it.

2. Pick up the Gold candle, hold it up and say,

"I call forth the Alchemy of the Heavenly Realms, to bring abundance and prosperity from higher dimensions to fill my life and my hands." Place the gold candle back on the grid and light it.

3. Pick up the red candle, hold it up and say,

"I call forth the Red Life Force from the Earthly Realm to fill my life and my hands with the abundance and prosperity, passion and strength, wealth, health and comfort." Place the red candle back on the grid and light it.

5. Now go to the four Goddesses around the square, one by one, pick up the votive or tea candle and say,

"I call forth Goddess (name of Goddess) to bring forth (state intention)." Place each candle back in its position and light it.

6. Now go to each of the 9 Goddesses around the circle and pick up each candle in turn and say,

"I call forth Goddess (name of Goddess) to bring forth (state intention)." Place each candle back in its position and light it. When the votives burn out and you start new candles, you can make new intentions or gain momentum with the same intentions.

Print all your intentions on a piece of paper and place them by the candle grid and say them each time you light the grid.

Continue to light this grid for the entire month or for a three-month phase. This grid will create greater flow of energy to bring abundance and prosperity. The energies of the thirteen aspects of the

Divine Mother wafting in the immediate environment, as you work and live everyday is great abundance in itself.

For information on how to purchase crystal clusters for this grid, go to Infinite Light Crystal Gallery on www.wavesofbliss.com. I will charge each of these with the Divine Mother and the thirteen Goddesses in your name and for your special intentions, to increase the magnifying power of your grid. Each of the points of the cluster can represent an aspect of the Divine Mother.

If you have your own favorite clear quartz or rose quartz piece, feel free to use it instead. I have explained how to charge your own piece to use with this grid in the summary section.

Channeling Index

Chapter I: Release Betrayal and Restore God-Unity
Template for Release of Betrayal, Bondage, Enslavement and the Union of Twin Flames to Bring Joy and God-Unity
- Used in January 2007 newsletter
- Archangel Michael, channeled January 16, 2007

Chapter II: The Golden Throne
Receiving the Blueprint of Divine Will in the Presence of the Golden Throne
- Used in the February 2007 Newsletter
- Jeshua Ben Joseph, channeled January 16, 2007

Chapter III: Karma and Karmic Entanglement
Release of Karma and Karmic Entanglements to Realize our Divinely Ordained Mission
- Used in March 2007 Newsletter
- Hecate, channeled January 23, 2007

Chapter IV: Releasing Negativity
Releasing Negative Energies to Gain Higher Light
- Used in April 2007 Newsletter
- St. Germain, channeled April 29, 2006

CHAPTER V: TRUTH AND NEGATIVITY
FINDING TRUTH THROUGH THE
RELEASE OF NEGATIVITY AT GLOBAL SCALE
- Used in May 2007 Newsletter
- Metatron, channeled March 29, 2007

CHAPTER VI: FORGIVENESS
PRAYER FOR FORGIVENESS AND
RELEASE OF KARMIC ENTANGLEMENTS
- Used in June 2007 Newsletter
- Metatron, channeled January 21, 2005

CHAPTER VII: REJUVENATION
MERGING THE RED LIFE FORCE ENERGY OF EARTH
WITH PURE WHITE LIGHT AND EMBRACING
THE FEMININE CREATIVE FORCE
- Used in July 2007 Newsletter
- Metatron, channeled April 26, 2007

CHAPTER VIII: PARAMATMAN LIGHT
CALLING FOR THE DESCENT OF PARAMATMAN LIGHT
TO CLEANS EARTH AND THE FIVE ELEMENTS
- Used in August 2007 newsletter
- Metatron, channeled January 12, 2005

Chapter IX: Alchemy of Healing, Protection and Manifestation
Alchemical Grid for Healing, Protection
and Manifestation with Mother Mary, Quan Yin,
Archangels Michael, Metatron, Uriel and Raphael
- Used in September 2007 Newsletter
- Metatron, channeled January 13, 2006

Chapter X: Lords of Light and the Creative Force
Invoking the Lords of Light and
Clearing the Five Body System
to embrace the Creative Force of Divine Mother
- Used in October 2007 Newsletter
- Metatron, channeled February 2007

Chapter XI: Protection and Transmutation
Grid of Light for Release of Anger, Fear,
Pain and Struggle
- Used in April, Special Edition, Newsletter
- Metatron, channeled April 9, 2007

Chapter XII: Abundance and Prosperity
The Divine Mother's Prosperity
and Abundance Magnification Grid of Light
- Used in August 2008 Newsletter
- Divine Mother, channeled July 15, 2008 and Hecate,
  channeled January 15, 2007

BIBLIOGRAPHY

Bailey, Alice. *Initiations Human and Solar.* Lucis Publishing Company, 1997

Bailey, Alice. *The Rays and The Initiations, vol. 5.* Lucis Publishing Company, 1971

Blavatsky, Helena Petrovna. *The Secret Doctrine.*
Theosophical University Press, 1888

Burnham, Sophy. *A Book of Angels.* Ballantine Books, 1990

Doreal. *The Emerald Tablets of Thoth the Atlantean.* Source Books, Inc., 2002

Freke, Timothy and Gandy, Peter. *The Hermetica: The Lost Wisdom of the Pharaohs.* Penguin Group, 1999

Grattan, Brian. *Mahatma I and II: The I Am Presence.*
Light Technology Publishing, 1994

Guiley, Rosemary Ellen. *Encyclopedia of Angels. 2nd Edition.*
Checkmark Books, 2004

Haich, Elisabeth. *Initiation.* Aurora Press, Incorporated, 2000

Hurtack, James J. *The Keys of Enoch.* Academy for Future Science,
Los Gatos, CA, 2004

Kaplan, Areh. *Sefer Yetzirah: The Book of Creation.*
Rev. Ed. Samuel Weiser, 1997

King, Godfrey Ray. *I Am Discourses of St. Germain Vol 1-20.*
St. Germain Foundation, 2007

Lewis, James R. and Evelyn Dorothy Oliver. *Angels A to Z.*
Visible Ink Press, 1996

MC Clure, Janet. *Sanat Kumara: Training a Planetary Logos (Tools for Transformation).* Light Technology Publishing, 1990

Meera, Mother. *Answers Part I and II.*
Mother Meera Publications, Germany, 1991

Printz, Thomas. *The Seven Beloved Archangels Speak.*
Ascended Masters Teaching Foundation, 1986

Printz, Thomas. *The Seven Mighty Elohim Speak on: The Seven Steps to Precipitation.*
Ascended Masters Teaching Foundation, 1986

Prophet, Mark and Elizabeth Clare. *Lords of the Seven Rays.*
Summit University Press, Corwin Springs, MT, 1986.

Prophet, Elizabeth Clare. *Soul Mates and Twin Flames.*
Summit University Press, Corwin Springs, MT, 1999

Prophet, Mark and Elizabeth Clare. *The Masters and their Retreats.*
Summit University Press, Corwin Springs, MT, 2003

Safai, Nasrin. *Path to Enlightenment, The Pillar of Light, Book I.*
Waves of Bliss Publishing, 2008

Safai, Nasrin. *Gifts of Practical Guidance for Daily Living: Healing, Protection,
Manifestation, Enlightenment – Gifts II.* Waves of Bliss Publishing, 2005

Safai, Nasrin. *Gifts from the Masters of Light: Journeys Into the Inner Realms of
Consciousness – Gifts III.* Waves of Bliss Publishing, 2005

Safai, Nasrin. *Gifts of Wisdom and Truth from the Masters of Light: Tools for Clearing,
Release, Abundance and Empowerment – Gifts IV.* Waves of Bliss Publishing, 2005

Stearn, Jess. *Edgar Cayce: The Sleeping Prophet.* Bantam, 1989

Szekely, Edmond-Bordeaux. *Essene Gospel of Peace.* I.B.S. International, 1981

Walsh, Neale Donald. *Complete Conversations with God, Volumes 1-3.*
Penguin Group, 2005

Walsh, Neale Donald. *Friendship with God.* Penguin Group, 2002

Walsh, Neale Donald. *Communion with God.* Penguin Group, 2007

ORGANIZATION WEBSITES FOR RELATED INFORMATION

www.amma.org

www.karunamayi.org

www.mmdarshanamerica.com

www.share-international.org

www.waynepeterson.com

www.yantradesigngroup.com

www.wakeupcompany.com

www.edgarcayce.org

www.nasrinsafai.com

www.wavesofbliss.com

www.godunity.org

www.path-to-enlightenment.com

ACKNOWLEDGEMENTS

*I offer thanks to all beings and all people
who have contributed to bring these books to life.*

With great love, I thank the following people for their contributions.

*To Patsy Balacchi of Yantra Design Group for her creative design skills,
cover design, photography and her joy of creating perfection.*

To Jane A. Matthews for her publishing and editing skills.

*To James Foster for his invaluable participation in all Phases
and for his gentle and constructive delivery of advice.*

To Kathy Rowshan for the reviews and corrections of numerous drafts.

*To Michael Kopel, The webmaster for Waves of Bliss and Path-to-enlightenment
websites and for his diligence in keeping archives of the endless hours of channeled
teachings in sound and written forms. To Theresa Martin for diagram design.*

*For invaluable comments and editing remarks
I thank Allen Blanchard, Hara Weaver and Sunny Alavi.*

To Tom Campell of King Printing and Adi Books.

To Dr John Alderson and Shabnam Sadr for their loving support.

*Finally, I thank everyone who contributed by participating in
channeling sessions where we received the information contained in this book.*

ABOUT THE AUTHOR

Nasrin is an internationally known channel of the Ascended Masters and Angelic Beings of Light. In 1999, Lord Metatron requested of Nasrin to conduct channeled life readings to aid those souls who are drawn to find their life's mission and to recall their lineage of Light.

Part of her life's mission is to travel the world anchoring ascension energies of Light at locations on all continents through ceremonies, sacred dances, mantras, prayers and invocations given by the Masters. Nasrin has been a channel for Metatron, Melchizedek, Sanat Kumara, Archangel Michael, Uriel, Raphael, Jesus, Mother Mary, Buddha, St. Germain, Quan Yin, Hecate, Athena, Red Feather and other Ascended Beings of Light.

She attended Chelsea School of Art in London, received a Bachelors Degree from the University of Decorative Arts in Tehran, a Masters Degree in Environmental Planning from Nottingham University in England and did her Doctoral Studies in the role of women in the development of the third world. She has taught at Harvard University and universities and institutes of higher education around the world. Presently she holds the post of Professor of Esoteric Spirituality at Universal Seminary, where materials from her books are taught for college credit.

Nasrin is the founder of the Foundation for the Attainment of God-Unity (FAGU), an educational and holistic healing organization which provides classes, workshops, books and support materials for spiritual practice open to all. All proceeds from the sale of this book support the work of the Masters through FAGU (www.godunity.org).

OTHER BOOKS BY NASRIN SAFAI

Path to Enlightenment, Book II, Waves of Bliss Publishing 2008

Path to Enlightenment, Book III, Waves of Bliss Publishing 2008

Gifts from Ascended Beings of Light: Prayers, Meditations, Mantras and Journeys for Soul Growth — Gifts I, Agapi Publishing, 2003.

Gifts of Practical Guidance for Daily Living: Healing, Protection, Manifestation, Enlightenment — Gifts II, Waves of Bliss Publishing, 2005.

Gifts from the Masters of Light: Journeys Into the Inner Realms of Consciousness — Gifts III, Waves of Bliss Publishing, 2005.

Gifts of Wisdom and Truth from the Masters of Light: Tools for Clearing, Release, Abundance and Empowerment — Gifts IV, Waves of Bliss Publishing, 2005.

To purchase a book, visit www.wavesofbliss.com/books or email Nasrin@wavesofbliss.com

To subscribe to our free newsletter, go to www.wavesofbliss.com.

To read more on Path to Enlightenment news, go to www.path-to-enlightenment.com